Contents

Essentials

MARINADES
1 Marinade 1
2 Marinade 2
3 Marinade 3

BATTERS
4 Basic Batter for Deep-frying
5 Basic Batter for Crêpes

STUFFINGS
6 Stuffing 1
7 Stuffing 2

BASIC BUTTERS
8 Garlic Butter
9 Shallot Butter
10 Salmon Butter
11 Anchovy Butter
12 Kneaded Butter
   (Manié Butter)
13 *Technique: How to Clarify Butter*

Basic Stocks

14 *Technique: How to Clarify Broth or Consommé*
15 Basic Brown Beef Stock 1
16 Basic Brown Beef Stock 2
17 Basic Chicken Stock 1
18 Basic Chicken Stock 2
19 Basic Fish Stock
   (Court Bouillon)
20 Basic Vegetable Stock

Basic Sauces

21 An Explanation of "Roux"
22 *Technique How to make a White Roux*
23 *Technique: How to make a Brown Roux*

WHITE SAUCES
24 Basic White Sauce
   (Béchamel) - Thin
25 Basic White Sauce
   (Béchamel) - Thick
26 Basic White Sauce made
   with Chicken Stock
27 Basic Fish Sauce

BROWN SAUCES
28 Basic Brown Sauce - Thin
29 Basic Brown Sauce - Thick
30 Bourguignon Sauce
31 Devilled Sauce
32 Brown Mushroom Sauce

BASIC TOMATO SAUCE
33 Quick Tomato Sauce

EGG SAUCES
34 Béarnaise Sauce
35 Hollandaise Sauce

36 Mousseline Sauce

COLD SAUCES
37 French Dressing or
Vinaigrette
38 French Dressing with Garlic
39 French Dressing with Ailloli
40 Roquefort Dressing
41 Mayonnaise
42 Green Mayonnaise
43 Plum Sauce

Finger Food
COLD HORS D'OEUVRE
44 Shrimp on Toast
45 Cocktail Mushroom Caps
46 Vegetables à la Grecque
47 Roquefort Cheese Canapés
48 Smoked Salmon Canapés
49 Ailloli on Toast

HOT HORS D'OEUVRE
50 Croque Monsieur
51 Water Chestnuts à la Diable
52 Butterfly Shrimp
53 Mushroom Caps Stuffed
with Crab Meat
54 Mushroom Caps Stuffed
with Spinach and Ham

Entrées
COLD ENTREES
55 Halibut Served on Lettuce
Hearts
56 Scampi served in a Scallop
Shell
57 Avocado à la Martin
58 Garden Cantaloupe

HOT ENTRÉES
59 Snails Provençale
60 Snails au Gratin
61 Snails Bourguignon
62 Crêpes Stuffed with Shrimp
63 Coquilles St. Jacques
64 Brochettes of Scampi
65 Baked Oysters au Gratin
66 Mussels à la Crème

Soups
CREAM SOUPS
Thickened with Flour
67 Cream of Asparagus Soup
68 Cream of Mushroom Soup
69 Cream of Cucumber Soup
70 Cream of Tomato Soup

CREAM SOUPS
Thickened with Potato
71 Parmentier Cream Soup
72 Cream of Leek Soup
73 Cream of Carrot Soup

CLEAR SOUPS
74 Vegetable Soup
75 Onion Soup au Gratin

76 CLAM CHOWDER
COLD SOUPS
77 Vichyssoise
78 Gazpacho

Beautiful Eggs
79 Eggs à la Française
80 Eggs with Cream

Many cuts of beef are suitable for roasting, but the tastiest cut is the rib roast — the ribs give the meat an excellent flavor. However, it is also one of the more expensive cuts. A good cut of beef should be aged by your butcher for 2 to 3 weeks. The aging process increases the tenderness and the flavor.

Pol Martin

The Art of Cooking
The French Way

DOLPHIN BOOKS
Doubleday and Company, Inc.
GARDEN CITY, NEW YORK

Dolphin edition: 1975
ISBN: 0-385-04699-5
Library of Congress Catalog Card Number: 74-33739
All Rights Reserved
Printed in Canada

81 Scrambled Eggs
82 Eggs Chasseur
83 Eggs Orientale
84 The Art of Omelette
85 Cheese Omelette
86 Mushroom Omelette

Economical Dishes
87 Beef Sautéed with Onions
88 Mushrooms à la Crème
    on Toast
89 Macaroni à la Barbara
90 Roast Beef à l'Italienne
91 One for Three
92 Halibut Casserole
93 Hamburger à la Ritz
94 Quiche Maison
95 Saucisses à l'Italienne

Soufflés & Fondues
96 Cheese Soufflé
97 Potato Soufflé
98 Party Beef Fondue
99 Cheese Fondue

Fish & Crustaceans
FISH
100 Lake Trout Baked in Foil
101 Pickerel à la Coker
102 Fillet of Perch with
     Mushrooms
103 Lake Trout Amandine
104 Salmon Poached in Court
     Bouillon
105 Poached Salmon with
     Mousseline Sauce
106 Poached Halibut with
     Mushroom Sauce
107 Cod au Gratin
108 Cod à l'Espagnole
109 Broiled Fillet of Porgy with
     Shallot Butter
110 Sole Bretonne

CRUSTANCEANS
111 *Technique: How to cook Shrimp*
112 Lobster Newburg
113 Lobster à la Lincoln
114 Shrimp Provençale
115 Scampi au Gratin
116 Alaska Crab Legs
117 Frog's Legs Provençale

Meat & Fowl
BEEF
118 *Technique: How to Roast Beef*
119 Club Steak Bordelaise
120 Steak, Chinese Style
121 Club Steak au Poivre
122 Club Steak à la Halna
123 Top Round Strogonoff
124 Braised Short Ribs
125 Boeuf Bourguignon
126 Stuffed Beef Flank
127 Stuffed Cabbage Rolls
128 Brochettes of Beef

CHICKEN
129 Coq au Vin
130 Chicken Casserole
131 Chicken Kiev
132 Chicken Arlesienne
133 Chicken New Orleans
134 Everyday Chicken
135 Chicken à la Point
136 Roast Chicken

137 Duck à la Stanley Park
138 Lamb Shish Kebabs

PORK
139 Roast Loin of Pork
140 Stuffed Pork Tenderloin
141 Pork Chops à la Diable

VEAL
142 Veal Scaloppine Printanière
143 Veal Chops with Artichoke
    Hearts
144 Blanquette of Veal
145 Stuffed Paupiettes of Veal
146 Croquettes of Veal

VARIETY MEATS
147 *Technique: Preparation of*
    Sweetbreads
148 Braised Sweetbreads
149 Grilled Sweetbreads
    with Béarnaise Sauce
    and Watercress
150 Veal Kidneys with Madeira
    Wine
151 *Technique: Preparation of*
    Calf's Brains
152 Calf's Brains with Capers
153 Calf's Liver, English Style
154 Calf's Liver Bergerac
155 Calf's Liver on Skewers

Rice
156 Rice Pilaf
157 Rice à l'Egyptienne
158 Rice à la Grecque
159 Rice, Chinese Style

Vegetables
SALADS
160 Caesar Salad
161 The Everyday Salad
162 Pol's Potato Salad
163 Tomato Salad

HOT VEGETABLES
164 Fresh Beans
165 Braised Endives
166 Mushrooms Provençale
167 Duchess Potatoes
168 Lyonnaise Potatoes
169 Parisenne Potatoes
170 Zucchini, Italian Style

Desserts
BASIC DOUGHS
171 Basic Pie Dough
172 Basic Sweet Dough
173 Creampuff Dough
CREAMS
174 Pastry Cream
175 Thick Custard Cream
176 Chantilly Cream
177 Chocolate Sauce
DESSERTS
178 Iced Banana Soufflé
179 Caramel Custard
180 Cherries Jubliee
181 Chocolate Quatre Quart
182 Peach Melba
183 Pears Hélène
184 Hot Sabayon
185 Zambia fruit salad
186 Zog's baked Alaska

6

Introduction

Like my television program, this cookbook is about the technique of cooking. Once you know the technique of cooking you can easily adapt recipes to your own taste. It will be simple for you to add other ingredients or make changes according to what you have in your kitchen. For example, the basic technique to make cream soup of flour plus liquid plus vegetable stays the same. The only thing that changes is the vegetable you want to use -- cucumber, tomato, lettuce, etc. The sautéeing of fish filets is another example of having one technique which may be adapted to produce a variety of dishes. The filet is always dipped in milk and flour and sautéed in butter or margarine or vegetable oil, and the garnish is added to easily become either *meunier* or a *provençale*.

My idea of a living nightmare is a kitchen full of pots and pans that stick and burn, knives that refuse to cut and a clutter of gadgets that fail to live up to their claims. In my dream, I would gather these fiendish utensils together, dispose of them rudely and start anew. Of course, this is not a very realistic solution in real life, but we should take a critical look at our equipment and see if a few changes and additions would help the situation in our kitchens.

Pots and Pans

Let's look at the pots and pans first. They should be like good friends -- well chosen, trustworthy, predictable and enduring. A heavy bottomed pan or pot lets you cook slowly without scorching; it conducts and distributes the heat evenly. It should be easy to clean, have a practical shape and be pleasant to look at.

These qualities can be found in many different materials. First, there is the heavy restaurant-type copper pan (the Rolls Royce of the kitchen) that offers superb performance and costs a great deal. This pot will last for generations -- you can even include it in your will.

You can also choose heavy enamelled cast iron; it comes in a large choice of colors to cheer your kitchen.

Another good choice would be stainless steel with copper bottom, providing the copper layer is substantial. There is also stainless steel with aluminum bottoms.

Thick aluminum is a very good choice as the handle can go in the oven. They will, however, discolor egg sauces.

Plain cast iron is also good but needs prompt attention after using to avoid rusting.

How many pots and pans?

There is, I believe, always the ideal tool for any particular job. However, one can certainly work with a minimum of well-chosen pots and pans until the need arises for adding to the collection.

MUST HAVES:

1 or 2 oval or round casseroles (*used for stews, braises, etc.*)
-- 10" to 12" casseroles will hold food enough for 4 to 6 persons
-- the lid should be tight fitting
-- bottoms must be burner-proof and handles must be oven-proof

2 small deep saucepans with covers and heavy bottoms (*used for sauces, boiling down liquids, etc.*)

1 larger, deep-sided saucepan with cover (*used for some of the soups, boiling vegetables, rice, etc.*)

1 sauté pan with cover and long oven-proof handle (*used for browning food on the burner and finishing in the oven, for sautéing steaks, chops, etc,*)
generally 10" to 12" diameter for 4 persons

1 roasting pan

COULD ADD:

-- omelette pan
-- heavy bottomed skillet with sloping sides
-- deep fryer
-- fish poacher

Knives

How many knives? Carbon steel knives can be sharpened quickly and retain an edge longest but need more attention in cleaning.

How to Chop

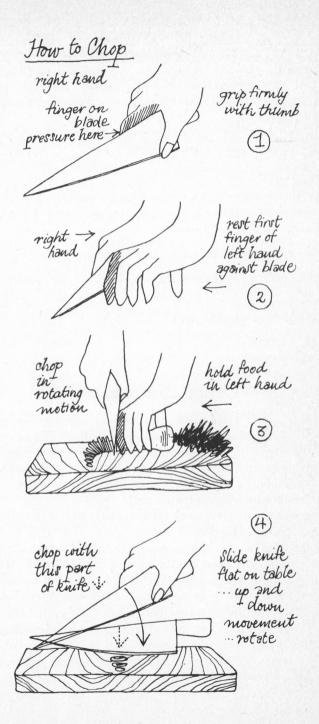

right hand

finger on
blade
pressure here →

grip firmly
with thumb

①

right
hand →

rest first
finger of
left hand
against blade

←

②

chop
in
rotating
motion

hold food
in left hand

←

③

④

chop with
this part
of knife ↓↓

slide knife
flat on table
...up and
↑ down
movement
...rotate

They will rust and stain unless cleaned and well dried right after every use.

The stainless steel knife looks well and has a good cutting edge. It needs only ordinary attention in cleaning but must be sharpened often.

Some handles are dishwasher-proof; find out before you put them into water that may be too hot.

MUST HAVE

1 10" chef knife -- with a straight blade, wide at the handle and tapering to a point. (*used for chopping and dicing vegetables and cutting raw meat and chicken, etc.*)

1 small paring knife for peeling, cutting and mincing.

1 slicing knife with long straight thin blade

1 knife sharpener
1 chef's knife in stainless steel

COULD ADD:
1 8" chef knife

Other Paraphernalia

The whisk is such a versatile tool for stirring and beating! The 10" stainless steel piano wire whisk with wooden or stainless steel handle is the most all-purpose of the wide size range available. One could also make good use of a large balloon whip for egg whites, etc., a large hard wire whip for mashed potatoes and a small piano wire whip for certain sauces.

The strainer or sieve is a very neccessary tool. Try to find one in stainless steel as it doesn't rust.

A food mill is not a must as your sieve can sometimes do the same job. But the good food mills have at least 3 disks, for fine, medium, and coarse puréeing. This lets you puré soups, fruits and vegetables as well as many cooked leftovers. It can be a real dollar saver and there are recipes that call for its use. (This tool is not to be confused with a food grinder that handles mainly dry foods.)

Two rubber spatulas and two wooden spoons will see you through any meal preparation.

Serving Dishes and Platters

I like to present my food on large stainless steel platters for practical reasons. After arranging the food on the platter, it can be kept hot in the oven while any other last minute preparations are done. Oven-proof porcelain and earthenware dishes and platters are also available.

Work Surface

Cutting or chopping on counter tops or on stainless steel will ruin your knives not to mention your counter top.

The best cutting surface is still wood; your best chopping boards are made from laminated maple. Every kitchen, no matter how small, needs one.

To keep the board fresh and sanitary is simple. After using, remove any remaining food. Now sprinkle the board with any chlorine-type powdered cleanser and wipe clean with a damp cloth. In this way the chlorine will sanitize the surface without leaving any odor.

Herbs and Spices

The matter of seasoning and taste is a very personal thing. I can only outline how I like to use herbs and spices and urge you to make more use of them in your day-to-day cooking. Some combinations are traditional while others are simply personal preference.

BLACK PEPPER: stronger than white pepper because the shell of the peppercorn has not been removed. If you are really fond of pepper, you will want to grind your own peppercorns in a pepper mill. (An inexpensive mill is never a bargin as it will only last a short time before wearing out.)

WHITE PEPPER: a little milder than black pepper. Used in white sauces and whenever you don't want black specks showing. Like black pepper, it loses some of its flavor when ground ahead of time.

PAPRIKA: (Spanish pepper) comes from the red pimento. Used mainly for goulash, chicken and some of the stronger sauces. Adds colour without being too hot.

CAYENNE PEPPER: very hot; comes from the pimento. Should

be used in very small quantities for stew and sauces.

NUTMEG: more flavorful if bought whole and grated as needed. Used in many dishes. Try a little in white sauce or mashed potatoes.

MUSTARD: dry English mustard and French paste. Used in cold and hot sauces and dressings.

BAYLEAF*: used in almost any soup. Lovely in stews, court bouillon, fish, etc.

THYME*: used mainly with meat, bouillon and soups. A stronger than average herb -- you don't need much to flavor a dish.

TARRAGON: used with vinegar, mustard and some dishes with sauces such as Chicken Tarragon. Also used in court bouillon. Try a little in your salad dressing.

CHERVIL: a "fines herb"; use as with parsley for a delicate flavor. A favorite in sauces, omelettes and soups.

ROSEMARY: used with meat, some sauces.

SAGE: used for stuffing and brings out the best in wild game.

BASIL*: used for meat and sauces.

SALT: if sea salt is used it must be ground in a mill. The mill should have a grinder made of heavy bakelite to prevent corrosion in humid weather.

Cooking Tips

USING WINES, BEER AND SPIRITS: Both red and white wine are used in cooking. They should be strong and dry. Sweet wines are rarely used in cooking.

Most recipes calling for dry wine can have beer as a substitute. In the same way, you can always substitute beef or chicken stock and produce a very satisfactory dish.

When you flambé brandy, cognac, etc., it is important that not only do you set the liquor aflame, but reduce the quantity slightly by evaporation to remove the raw taste of alcohol.

USING MUSTARD IN COOKING: never add it to a sauce until just before serving. If it cooks in the sauce it will give a bitter taste.

*Bouquet garni consists of these herbs plus parsley and celery added to a dish in a parcel so they can easily be found and removed later. Traditionally, all were tied together in a little cheesecloth bag. A simple way is to sandwich the parsley and herbs between two pieces of celery and tie with string.

The Recipes

Marinades

1
Marinade 1

This marinade is ideal for beef, veal or chicken. Its purpose is to enhance the flavor of the meat and make it more tender; therefore, I suggest that you use economical cuts of meat.

You can cook the meat in this marinade, especially for such dishes as "boeuf bourguignon" or "coq au vin."

The marinade can also be used in the preparation of sauces and for basting barbecued brochettes of beef.

> BEEF, VEAL OF CHICKEN*
> DRY RED OR WHITE WINE
> 1/4 TEASPOON THYME
> 2 BAY LEAVES
> 2 WHOLE CLOVES
> 20 WHOLE PEPPERCORNS
> 1 TEASPOON CHERVIL [OPTIONAL]
> 2 GARLIC CLOVES, SMASHED [OPTIONAL]
> FRESHLY GROUND PEPPER
> 1 CARROT, PEELED AND THINLY SLICED
> 1 ONION, PEELED AND THINLY SLICED
> 3 TABLESPOONS VEGETABLE OIL

Place the meat in a bowl and add wine to cover.

Add the remaining ingredients.

Cover the meat with wax paper and refrigerate for at least 12 hours.

This marinade will keep, refrigerated, for 48 hours.

*Average portions: *beef or veal,* 1/2 pound per person; *chicken,* 1/2 chicken per person.

2
Marinade 2

This marinade is used in the preparation of lamb shish-kebabs.
  When you barbecue, you can use the marinade to baste the shish-kebabs.

---

2 POUNDS LAMB FROM THE LOIN OR THE SHOULDER*
  CUT INTO 1 INCH CUBES
1 CUP VEGETABLE OIL OR OLIVE OIL
  JUICE OF 1½ LEMONS
½ CUP DRY WHITE WINE
1 GARLIC CLOVE SMASHED
16 WHOLE PEPPERCORNS
¼ TEASPOON THYME
2 BAY LEAVES
1 TEASPOON CHERVIL
¼ TEASPOON PAPRIKA
1 TEASPOON TARRAGON
1 CARROT, PEELED AND THINLY SLICED
1 ONION, PEELED AND THINLY SLICED
  SALT

Combine all the ingredients, including the lamb, in a large bowl.

Cover the lamb with wax paper and refrigerate for at least 12 hours.

This marinade will keep, refrigerated, for 48 hours.

*Average portion: ½ pound lamb per person.

3
Marinade 3

This marinade is used for Barbecue chicken.

When you barbecue, you should baste the chicken with the marinade.

2	POUND CHICKEN, CUT IN TWO*
	PAPRIKA
2	GARLIC CLOVES, SMASHED AND FINELY CHOPPED
	JUICE OF 1 LEMON
½	CUP VEGETABLE OIL†
¼	TEASPOON THYME
2	BAY LEAVES
1	TEASPOON TARRAGON
	SALT
	FRESHLY GROUND PEPPER

Place the chicken halves in a stainless steel tray or platter.

Season the chicken with salt and pepper.

Sprinkle the chicken with paprika and cover the chicken with the remaining ingredients.

Cover the chicken with wax paper, refrigerate and marinate for at least two hours.

This marinade will keep, refrigerated, for 12 hours.

---

*Average portion: ½ chicken per person.

†You can use olive oil instead of vegetable oil; however, this will alter the flavor of the marinade.

Batters

4
Basic Batter for Deep-frying

This batter is ideal for:

> small squares of zucchini
> celery hearts
> small, whole carrots
> water chestnuts
> asparagus tips
> shrimp, etc.

1	CUP ALL PURPOSE FLOUR
1/4	TEASPOON SALT
2	TABLESPOONS VEGETABLE OIL
1 1/2	CUPS, LESS 3 TABLESPOONS COLD WATER
2	EGG WHITES

In a mixing bowl, combine the flour and the salt and then add the vegetable oil and the cold water. Blend well.

Refrigerate the mixture, uncovered, for 30 minutes.

Beat the egg whites until very stiff.
Remove the batter from the refrigerator.
Gently but thoroughly fold the egg whites into the batter.

5
Basic Crêpe Batter
Yield: 20 crêpes

---

1   CUP ALL PURPOSE FLOUR, SIFTED
½   TEASPOON SALT
4   LARGE EGGS
1¼ CUPS LIQUID [HALF MILK AND HALF WATER]
5   TABLESPOONS CLARIFIED BUTTER, MELTED,
     LUKEWARM
1   TEASPOON FRESH PARSLEY, FINELY CHOPPED

In a mixing bowl, combine the flour and the salt.

In a separate mixing bowl, lightly beat the eggs with a whisk and blend in the liquid.

Add the flour to the liquid and blend well, with a whisk.
The batter should have the consistency of heavy cream.

Add the clarified butter, in a thin stream, whisking constantly.

Strain the batter through a sieve and add the chopped parsley.

Technique ... *How to Make Crêpes*

Use an 8" steel crêpe pan

1) Melt 1 tablespoon butter in the crêpe pan over high heat.
2) Remove the pan from the heat.
3) Wipe off the excess butter with a paper towel.
4) Barely cover the bottom of the crêpe pan with batter.
5) Return the pan to the stove and cook the crêpe over high heat.

The crêpes should be paper thin.

Repeat steps 1 through 3 if the crêpes begin to stick.

The crêpes will keep for 3 months, wrapped in wax paper and frozen.

Crêpes

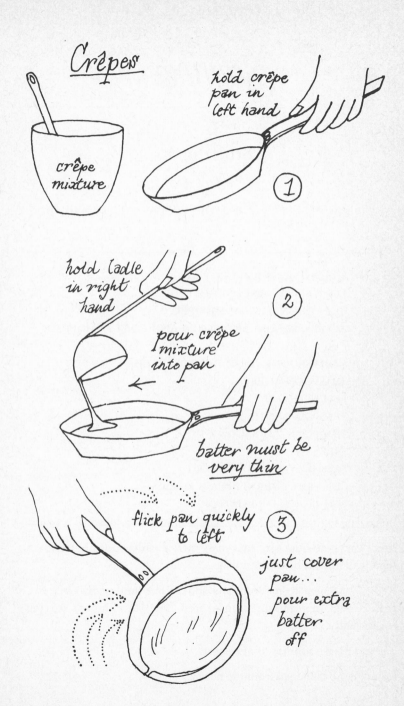

crêpe mixture

hold crêpe pan in left hand

①

hold ladle in right hand

②

pour crêpe mixture into pan

batter must be _very thin_

flick pan quickly to left

③

just cover pan... pour extra batter off

Stuffings

6
Stuffing 1

Yield: 2 cups

For poultry, beef or veal. This recipe produces enough stuffing for a 3 to 4 pound chicken.

3	TABLESPOONS BUTTER
½	CUP CELERY, FINELY CHOPPED
½	CUP ONION, FINELY CHOPPED
3	APPLES, PEELED AND CORED AND FINELY CHOPPED
2	DRIED SHALLOTS FINELY CHOPPED [OPTIONAL]
2	TABLESPOONS FRESH PARSLEY, FINELY CHOPPED
1	TEASPOON CHERVIL
1	PINCH THYME
½	TEASPOON SAGE
½	TEASPOON TARRAGON
	SALT
	FRESHLY GROUND PEPPER
1	CUP VERY COARSE BREADCRUMBS
1	EGG LIGHTLY BEATEN

In a heavy, medium size saucepan, melt 2 tablespoons butter over high heat until it begins to foam.

Reduce the heat to medium and add all but the last two ingredients. Cook this mixture, uncovered, for 15 minutes, stirring occasionally.

Correct the seasonings, if necessary.

Remove the saucepan from the heat.

Add the breadcrumbs, mix well and blend in the remaining table-spoon of butter and the beaten egg.

This stuffing will keep for 2 to 3 days, refrigerated and covered with buttered wax paper.

7
Stuffing 2

This stuffing is sufficient for a two pound dover sole, trout, doré or red snapper, etc.

---

3 TABLESPOONS BUTTER
1 POUND MUSHROOMS, WASHED AND FINELY
   CHOPPED
1 ONION, PEELED AND FINELY CHOPPED
2 TABLESPOONS FRESH PARSLEY, FINELY CHOPPED
1 TABLESPOON CHERVIL
1 PINCH THYME
  SALT
  FRESHLY GROUND PEPPER
¼ TEASPOON FENNEL
¼ CUP BREADCRUMBS
2 TABLESPOONS HEAVY CREAM [OR 1 BEATEN EGG]
2 DROPS TABASCO SAUCE

In a heavy, medium size saucepan, melt the butter over high heat until it begins to foam.

Reduce the heat to medium, add all the ingredients except for the last three and cook the mixture, uncovered, for 15 minutes, stirring frequently.

Correct the seasonings, if necessary.

Remove the saucepan from the heat and mix in the breadcrumbs, the cream (or beaten egg) and the tabasco sauce.

This stuffing can be made ahead of time and kept, refrigerated and covered with buttered wax paper, for 24 hours.

Basic Butters

8
Garlic Butter

This butter can be used on steaks, for barbecues, scampi, garlic bread and to prepare snails.

½	POUND UNSALTED BUTTER, AT ROOM TEMPERATURE
2	TABLESPOONS FRESH PARSLEY, FINELY CHOPPED
1	TEASPOON CHERVIL
4	TO 5 GARLIC CLOVES, SMASHED AND FINELY CHOPPED
	SALT
	FRESHLY GROUND PEPPER
1	TABLESPOON DRIED SHALLOT, FINELY CHOPPED
	JUICE OF ¼ LEMON

In a mixing bowl, blend all the ingredients together.

Correct seasonings, if necessary.

To store, roll in aluminium foil.

This butter will keep, frozen, for 3 months.

Garlic Butter

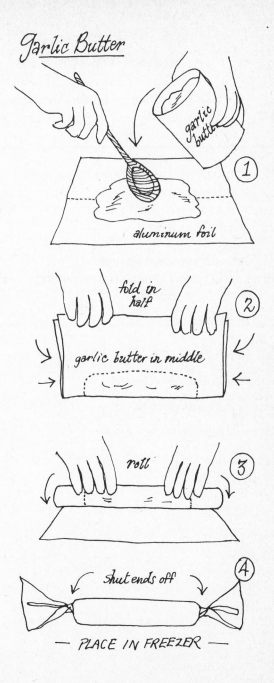

garlic butter

① aluminum foil

fold in half

② garlic butter in middle

roll ③

④ shut ends off

— PLACE IN FREEZER —

9
Shallot Butter

This butter is used for grilled or broiled steaks, barbecues and with fish.

½ POUND UNSALTED BUTTER AT ROOM
      TEMPERATURE
2 TABLESPOONS FRESH PARSLEY, FINELY CHOPPED
1 TEASPOON CHERVIL
    SALT
    FRESHLY GROUND PEPPER
2 TABLESPOONS DRIED SHALLOT, FINELY CHOPPED
    JUICE OF ¼ LEMON

In a mixing bowl, blend all the ingredients together.

Correct the seasonings, if necessary.

To store, roll in aluminium foil.

This butter will keep, frozen, for 3 months.

10
Salmon Butter

This butter is used for canapés and with grilled or broiled dover sole.

In French cookery, the great chefs use this butter to enhance the flavor of fish sauces.

¼ POUND [SCANT] SMOKED OR FRESH UNCOOKED SALMON
½ POUND UNSALTED BUTTER, AT ROOM
   TEMPERATURE
 I TEASPOON CHERVIL
   JUICE OF ¼ LEMON
   SMALL PINCH OF CAYENNE PEPPER
   SALT
   FRESHLY GROUND PEPPER

In a mortar, grind the salmon to a fine paste and strain it through a fine sieve.

If you do not have a mortar, mince the salmon at least twice with a meat grinder and then strain it through a fine sieve .

In a mixing bowl, thoroughly blend all the ingredients together.

Correct the seasonings, if necessary.

To store, roll in aluninium foil.

This butter will keep, frozen, for 3 months.

11
Anchovy Butter

This butter is used for canapés and for broiled, grilled or sautéed salmon steak.

2½ OUNCES ANCHOVY FILLETS
½ POUND UNSALTED BUTTER, AT ROOM
    TEMPERATURE
1 TEASPOON CHERVIL
JUICE OF ¼ LEMON
SMALL PINCH OF CAYENNE PEPPER
SALT
FRESHLY GROUND PEPPER

In a mortar, grind the anchovy fillets to a fine paste and strain them through a fine sieve.

If you do not have a mortar, mince the anchovy fillets at least twice with a meat grinder and then strain them through a fine sieve.

In a mixing bowl, thoroughly blend all the ingredients together.

Correct the seasonings, if necessary.

To store, roll in aluminium foil.

This butter will keep, frozen, for 3 months.

12
Kneaded Butter *(Manié Butter)*

This butter is used to thicken sauces.

---

2   TABLESPOONS BUTTER AT ROOM TEMPERATURE
1   TABLESPOON ALL PURPOSE FLOUR

Blend the butter and flour into a smooth paste.

13
Clarified Butter

Clarified butter is used to prepare "roux" and to sauté meat or vegetables. It will not burn as quickly as butter which has not been clarified.

Place one-half pound butter in a stainless steel bowl, or in the top part of a double boiler and set on top of a saucepan half-filled with almost boiling water, over very gentle heat.

The butter should not be touched. After it has melted, the impurities can be removed by:

a)   straining the butter through a cheesecloth, or
b)   cooling the butter. The whitish deposit will sink to the bottom of the receptacle and the clarified butter can easily be skimmed off.

This butter will keep, refrigerated, for approximately 2 weeks.

Basic Stocks

14
How to clarify consommé

To clarify 4 to 12 cups of consommé or broth:

Beef stock

COMBINE

   ½   **POUND GROUND BEEF**
   2   **EGG WHITES**
      SPICES OF YOUR CHOICE

Veal or chicken stock

COMBINE

   ½   **POUND GROUND VEAL OR CHICKEN**
   2   **EGG WHITES**
      SPICES OF YOUR CHOICE

Pour the mixture into the consommé or broth.

Bring to a boil, then simmer over very low heat.

All impurities will float to the surface and can easily be skimmed off.

15
Basic Brown Beef Stock 1

This stock is used to prepare brown sauces, French onion soup, braised beef, etc.

Cooking Time
2 TO 3 HOURS
1½ POUNDS BEEF [CHUCK OR SHANK]

6 TO 8 HOURS
3 POUNDS BONES [BEEF AND/OR VEAL]

BOUQUET GARNI CONSISTING OF
    ½ TEASPOON THYME
    2 BAY LEAVES
    1 TEASPOON CHERVIL
    ½ TEASPOON BASIL
    1 WHOLE CLOVE
    FRESH PARSLEY
    CELERY [SEE BASIC BROWN BEEF STOCK 2, *Recipe 16*]

2 MEDIUM SIZE CARROTS, COARSELY DICED
2 MEDIUM SIZE ONIONS, COARSELY DICED
2 CELERY STALKS, COARSELY DICED
  SALT
  FRESHLY GROUND PEPPER
2 MEDIUM SIZE ONIONS WITH THEIR SKIN,
  CUT IN TWO
2½ QUARTS WATER

Place the meat, or bones and the water in a stockpot, bring the liquid to a boil over high heat and skim.

Add the bouquet garni and all the vegetables except for the onions, which are cut in two, to the boiling liquid. Season with salt and pepper.

Place the two remaining onions, cut side down, in a hot cast iron sauté pan and cook, uncovered, until they become black. Drop the onions into the stock. The burned onions will give the stock its brown coloring.

Simmer the stock for the amount of time indicated above.

Strain the stock through a cheesecloth or a fine strainer.

This stock will keep, frozen, for 3 months.
This stock can be refrigerated, uncovered, for 7 to 10 days.

16
Basic Brown Beef Stock 2

Can be used for brown sauces, French onion soup, braised beef, etc.

    I BEEF BOUILLON CUBE
    4 CUPS BOILING WATER
      SALT
      FRESHLY GROUND PEPPER
      BOUQUET GARNI CONSISTING OF
  ¼ TEASPOON THYME
  ½ TEASPOON CHERVIL
    I BAY LEAF
  ¼ TEASPOON BASIL
    I WHOLE CLOVE
      FRESH PARSLEY
      CELERY

In a medium size saucepan, whisk the beef stock into the boiling water until well blended. Season, if necessary.

Add the bouquet garni and simmer the stock, uncovered, for 30 to 40 minutes.

Remove the bouquet garni and strain the stock through a cheese-cloth or a fine strainer.

This stock will keep, frozen, for 3 months.
This stock can be refrigerated, uncovered, for 7 to 10 days.

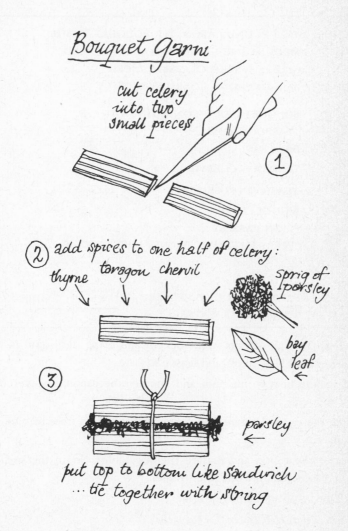

Bouquet garni

cut celery into two small pieces

①

② add spices to one half of celery:
thyme   tarragon   chervil   sprig of parsley

bay leaf

③

parsley

put top to bottom like sandwich
... tie together with string

17
Basic Chicken Stock 1

This stock can be used to prepare cream soups, white sauces, vegetable soups, etc.

1	TO 4 POUND CAPON, THOROUGHLY WASHED
2	MEDIUM SIZE CARROTS, COARSELY DICED
2	CELERY STALKS, COARSELY DICED
2	LARGE ONIONS, COARSELY DICED
	BOUQUET GARNI CONSISTING OF
½	TEASPOON THYME
2	BAY LEAVES
1	TEASPOON CHERVIL
½	TEASPOON ROSEMARY
1	WHOLE CLOVE
	FRESH PARSLEY
	CELERY [SEE BASIC BROWN BEEF STOCK 2, *Recipe 16*]
	SALT
	FRESHLY GROUND PEPPER
2½	TO 3 QUARTS WATER

Place all the ingredients in a stockpot and bring the liquid to a boil over high heat. Skim, and season to taste.

Reduce the heat to medium and simmer the capon, uncovered, for 2½ hours.

Pierce the capon's thigh. The capon is done if no trace of blood is apparent.

Remove the capon and discard the vegetables. Strain the stock through a cheesecloth or a fine strainer.

Cool the broth and remove the fat.

This stock will keep, frozen, for 3 months.
This stock can be refrigerated, uncovered, for 7 to 10 days.

18
Basic Chicken Stock 2

This stock is used for cream soups, white sauces, vegetable soups, etc.

```
 1  CHICKEN BOUILLON CUBE
 4  CUPS BOILING WATER
    SALT
    FRESHLY GROUND PEPPER
    BOUQUET GARNI CONSISTING OF
¼   TEASPOON THYME
 1  BAY LEAF
½   TEASPOON CHERVIL
¼   TEASPOON ROSEMARY
 1  WHOLE CLOVE
    FRESH PARSLEY
    CELERY [SEE BASIC BROWN BEEF STOCK 2, Recipe 16]
```

In a medium size saucepan, whisk the chicken stock into the boiling water until well blended.

Season the stock, if necessary.

Add the bouquet garni and simmer the stock, uncovered, for 30 to 40 minutes.

Strain the broth through a cheesecloth or a fine strainer.

This stock will keep, frozen, for 3 months.
This stock can be refrigerated, uncovered, for 7 to 10 days.

19
Basic Fish Stock (*Court Bouillon*)

This sauce is mainly used to prepare fish sauces, fish chowder, casseroles and to poach fish and crustaceans.

1	TABLESPOON BUTTER
2	POUNDS FISH BONES FROM WHITE, LEAN FISH
2	MEDIUM SIZE CARROTS, THINLY SLICED
1	LEEK, THINLY SLICED
2	MEDIUM SIZE ONIONS, THINLY SLICED
1	CELERY STALK, THINLY SLICED
20	MUSHROOMS, SLICED [OPTIONAL]
½	TEASPOON THYME
2	OR 3 BAY LEAVES
18	WHOLE PEPPERCORNS
2	WHOLE CLOVES
1	TEASPOON CHERVIL
	A FEW BRANCHES OF FRESH PARSLEY
½	TEASPOON TARRAGON
¼	TEASPOON FENNEL SEEDS
1½	CUPS DRY WHITE WINE, OR
	JUICE OF 1 LEMON OR
	3 TABLESPOONS WHITE VINEGAR
2½	QUARTS COLD WATER
	SALT
	FRESHLY GROUND PEPPER

In a large saucepan, melt the butter over high heat until it begins to foam. Reduce the heat to low, add the fish bones, the vegetables and the spices, cover and cook for 15 to 18 minutes.

Add the white wine (or lemon juice, or white vinegar) and the water. Season the liquid with salt and pepper.

Bring the liquid to a boil and simmer, uncovered, for 35 minutes.

Strain the court bouillon through a cheesecloth or a fine strainer.

This stock will keep, frozen, for 3 months.
This stock can be refrigerated, uncovered, for 3 to 4 days.

20
Basic Vegetable Stock

This stock is used to prepare cream soups, and vegetable soups.

1	TABLESPOON BUTTER
2	MEDIUM SIZE ONIONS, THINLY SLICED
2	MEDIUM SIZE CARROTS, THINLY SLICED
2	CELERY STALKS, THINLY SLICED
1	LEEK, THINLY SLICED
2½	QUARTS WATER
	SALT
	FRESHLY GROUND PEPPER
	BOUQUET GARNI CONSISTING OF
½	TEASPOON THYME
2	BAY LEAVES
½	TEASPOON BASIL
	FRESH PARSLEY
	CELERY [SEE BASIC BROWN BEEF STOCK 2, *Recipe 16*]

In a large saucepan, melt the butter over high heat until it begins to foam. Add all the vegetables, reduce the heat to low, cover and cook the vegetables for 10 minutes, stirring occasionally.

Add the water and the bouquet garni and season to taste with salt and pepper.

Bring the liquid to a boil over high heat, lower the heat to medium and simmer the stock, uncovered, for 35 to 40 minutes.

Strain the stock through a cheesecloth or a fine strainer.

This stock will keep, frozen, for 3 months.
This stock can be refrigerated and will keep, uncovered, for 7 to 10 days.

Basic Sauces

21
Roux

A roux is a mixture of butter or another fatty substance, and flour, which is used to thicken sauces and cream soups.

Amount of flour	Amount of fat*	Amount of Liquid	Yield†
1 TABLESPOON	1 TABLESPOON	1 CUP	⅔ CUP THIN SAUCE
1½ TABLESPOONS	1½ TABLESPOONS	1 CUP	⅔ CUP THICK SAUCE

Once a roux has been cooked, it will keep, refrigerated and covered, for 2 to 3 weeks.

It will also keep, frozen, for 3 months.

*butter, margarine, fat, roast meat drippings, etc.

†These proportions are based on a cooking time of 15 to 20 minutes.

22
White Roux

Melt the fat* in a small, heavy saucepan.

Add an equal amount of flour and cook over low heat, on top of the stove, for 4 minutes, stirring constantly with a wooden spoon.

The roux is cooked when it bubbles considerably.

*Butter, margarine, or roast chicken drippings.

23
Brown Roux

Preheat the oven to 250°.

Melt the fat* in a small, ovenproof casserole.
Mix in an equal amount of flour and cook over low heat, on top of the stove, for 4 minutes, stirring constantly with a wooden spoon.

Place the casserole in the oven and cook the roux, uncovered, stirring often.
The roux is cooked when it becomes a light brown color.
Do not let the flour burn.

*Butter, margarine, or roast chicken drippings.

White Sauces

24
Basic White Sauce *(Béchamel Sauce)* Thin

Yield: 3½ cups. Made with milk

This sauce is used in casserole dishes, fish dishes, pasta, macaroni and cheese.

4 TABLESPOONS BUTTER OR MARGARINE
4 TABLESPOONS FLOUR
4 CUPS HOT MILK
1 ONION, STUDDED WITH A WHOLE CLOVE
  SALT
  FRESHLY GROUND WHITE PEPPER
  DASH OF NUTMEG

In a heavy, medium size saucepan, melt the butter over high heat, until it begins to foam. Reduce the heat to medium, add the flour and cook the "roux", uncovered, for 5 minutes, stirring constantly.

Remove the saucepan from the stove and add one cup hot milk. Stir with a wooden spoon until well blended.

Reduce the heat to low, return the saucepan to the stove and add the rest of the hot milk, one cup at a time, stirring constantly.

Drop in the onion and season the sauce with salt, pepper and nutmeg. Simmer the sauce over low heat, uncovered, for 30 minutes, stirring occasionally.

Remove the onion before serving.

This sauce will keep for 2 days, covered with buttered wax paper and refrigerated. The wax paper must touch the surface of the sauce.

25
White Sauce *(Béchamel Sauce)* Thick
Yield: 3½ cups. Made with milk

This sauce is used in casserole dishes, fish dishes, pasta, macaroni and cheese.

6	TABLESPOONS BUTTER
6	TABLESPOONS FLOUR
4½	CUPS HOT MILK
1	ONION, STUDDED WITH A WHOLE CLOVE
	SALT
	FRESHLY GROUND WHITE PEPPER
	DASH OF NUTMEG

Follow the procedure outlined in Recipe 24, *Basic White Sauce -- Thin*

26
Basic White Sauce

Made with chicken stock, medium thickness. Yield: 3 cups

This sauce is used with chicken, for casserole dishes, vol-au-vent, and to prepare other sauces.

4	TABLESPOONS BUTTER
4	TABLESPOONS FLOUR
3½	CUPS HOT BASIC CHICKEN STOCK [*Recipes 17-18*]
½	CUP LIGHT CREAM
	SALT
	FRESHLY GROUND WHITE PEPPER
I	SMALL PINCH CAYENNE PEPPER
2	EGG YOLKS
I	TABLESPOON LIGHT CREAM

In a saucepan, melt the butter over high heat, until it begins to foam.

Reduce the heat to medium, add the flour, and cook the "roux", uncovered, for 5 minutes, stirring constantly with a wooden spoon.

Remove the saucepan from the heat and add one cup hot chicken stock. Stir with a wooden spoon until well blended.

Reduce the heat to low, return the saucepan to the stove and add the remaining chicken stock, one cup at a time, stirring constantly.

Add ½ cup cream and season the sauce to taste with salt, pepper and cayenne pepper.

Bring the sauce to a boil over high heat, reduce the heat to low and simmer the sauce, uncovered, for 30 minutes, stirring occasionally.

Remove the saucepan from the heat.

Before serving, combine the 2 egg yolks and 1 tablespoon light cream in a small mixing bowl. Blend the egg yolk and cream mixture into the sauce with a whisk and serve immediately.

The sauce, without the cream and egg yolk mixture, will keep for 2 days, covered with buttered wax paper and refrigerated. The wax paper must touch the surface of the sauce.

27
Basic Fish Sauce

Yield: 3½ cups

This sauce is served with white fish and used to prepare fish casseroles, coquilles St-Jacques, lobster Thermidor and lobster newburg.

4½ TABLESPOONS BUTTER
1 TABLESPOON DRIED SHALLOT, FINELY CHOPPED
1 CUP DRY WHITE WINE
4 TABLESPOONS FLOUR
4 CUPS HOT BASIC FISH STOCK [*Recipe 19*]
   SALT
   FRESHLY GROUND WHITE PEPPER
2 TABLESPOONS HEAVY CREAM [OPTIONAL]

In a heavy, medium size saucepan, melt ½ tablespoon butter over high heat, until it begins to foam. Reduce the heat to low, add the dry shallots and simmer, uncovered, for 2 minutes, stirring occasionally.

Add the wine to the shallots, and bring the liquid to a boil over high heat. Reduce the wine to one-third of its original volume.

At the same time, in a separate saucepan, melt the remaining 4 tablespoons butter over high heat, until the butter begins to foam. Reduce the heat to medium, add the flour and cook the "roux", uncovered, for 3 minutes, stirring constantly with a wooden spoon.

Remove the saucepan containing the "roux" from the stove and mix in one cup fish stock with a wooden spoon, until well blended. Reduce the heat to low. Return the saucepan to the heat and add the remaining fish stock, one cup at a time, stirring constantly. Add the reduced white wine to the sauce and season the sauce with salt and pepper. Bring the sauce to a boil over high heat, reduce the heat to low and simmer the sauce, uncovered, for 35 minutes, stirring occasionally. Strain.

Before serving, add 2 tablespoons heavy cream.

This sauce will keep for 2 days, covered with buttered wax paper and refrigerated. The wax paper must touch the surface of the sauce.

Brown Sauces

28
Basic Brown Sauce — Thin

Yield: 3½ cups

This basic sauce is used to prepare many other brown sauces and to prepare stews, boeuf bourguignon, etc.

4½ TABLESPOONS BUTTER OR MARGARINE OR BEEF
   DRIPPINGS

<pre>
 1   SMALL CARROT, DICED
 ½   STALK CELERY, DICED
 1   SMALL ONION, DICED
 1   PINCH THYME
 1   BAY LEAF
 ¼   TEASPOON CHERVIL
 4¼ TABLESPOONS ALL PURPOSE FLOUR
 4¼ CUPS HOT BASIC BROWN BEEF STOCK
     (Recipe 15-16)
     SALT
     FRESHLY GROUND PEPPER
</pre>

Preheat the oven to 250°.

In a small, heavy ovenproof casserole, melt the fat over high heat. Lower the heat to medium, add the diced vegetables and cook, uncovered, for 7 minutes, stirring frequently.

Add the spices and cook, uncovered, for 2 minutes, stirring occasionally.

Add the flour to the vegetables, mix well with a wooden spoon and place the casserole in the oven. Stir occasionally. Cook the mixture until the flour is golden brown.

Remove the casserole from the oven and let it cool for a few minutes.

Add one cup beef stock to the roux and mix in thoroughly with a wooden spoon. Return the casserole to the top of the stove, over low heat. Add the remaining beef stock, one cup at a time, while stirring constantly.

Bring the sauce to a boil over high heat and season to taste. Reduce the heat to low and simmer the sauce, uncovered, for 30 minutes.

This sauce will keep for one week, refrigerated and covered with buttered wax paper. The wax paper must touch the surface of the sauce.

29
Basic Brown Sauce — Thick

Yield: 3½ cups

This basic sauce is used to prepare many other brown sauces and used to cook stews, boeuf bourguignon, etc.

---

6 TABLESPOONS BUTTER OR MARGARINE OR ROAST
  BEEF DRIPPINGS
1 SMALL CARROT DICED
½ STALK CELERY DICED
1 SMALL ONION DICED
1 PINCH THYME
1 BAY LEAF
¼ TEASPOON CHERVIL
6 TABLESPOONS ALL PURPOSE FLOUR
4½ CUPS HOT BASIC BROWN BEEF STOCK [*Recipe 15-16*]
  SALT
  FRESHLY GROUND PEPPER

Prepare the sauce in the same manner as Recipe 28 (Basic Brown Sauce -- Thin)

30
Bourguignon Sauce

Yield: 2½ cups

Serve this sauce with fondue bourguignon, steaks, pork and veal chops, sweetbreads, stuffed mushroom crêpes, etc.

---

1 TEASPOON BUTTER
1 TABLESPOON DRIED SHALLOT, FINELY CHOPPED
FRESHLY GROUND PEPPER OR
   1 TEASPOON FRESH CHIVES, FINELY CHOPPED
2 CUPS DRY RED WINE
1 BAY LEAF
2 CUPS HOT BASIC BROWN SAUCE THICK [*Recipe 29*]
1 TABLESPOON FRESH PARSLEY FINELY CHOPPED

In a heavy, medium size saucepan, melt the butter over high heat until it begins to foam. Reduce the heat to medium, add the dry shallots and cook, uncovered, for 2 minutes, stirring occasionally.

Add the red wine, the pepper (or chives) and the bay leaf to the shallots.

Reduce the wine over high heat, to one-third of its original volume.

Add the brown sauce to the reduced wine, bring to a boil, and simmer the sauce, over very low heat, uncovered, for 20 minutes, stirring occasionally.

Remove the bay leaf and serve with the chopped parsley.

This sauce will keep for 2 to 3 days, covered with buttered wax paper and refrigerated. The wax paper must touch the surface of the sauce.

31
Devilled Sauce

Yield: 1¾ cups

Serve this sauce with pork chops, barbecued steaks, shish-kebabs, pork tenderloin.

6	OUNCES DRY WHITE WINE
3	TABLESPOONS WINE VINEGAR
2	TABLESPOONS DRIED SHALLOT, FINELY CHOPPED
½	TEASPOON FRESHLY GROUND PEPPER
2	CUPS HOT BASIC BROWN SAUCE THIN [*Recipe 28*]
	SALT
	DASH OF CAYENNE PEPPER
I	TABLESPOON FRESH PARSLEY, FINELY CHOPPED
I	TEASPOON FRESH CHIVES, FINELY CHOPPED
I	TEASPOON ENGLISH POWDERED MUSTARD
	JUICE OF ¼ LEMON

In a medium size saucepan, bring the wine, wine vinegar, dry shallots and pepper to a boil over high heat and reduce the liquid by two-thirds.

Add the brown sauce to the reduced wine and season to taste with salt, pepper and cayenne pepper.

Bring the sauce to a boil over high heat, reduce the heat to low and then simmer the sauce, uncovered, for 30 minutes, stirring occasionally.

Mix the parsley, the chives, the dry mustard and the lemon juice into the sauce.

This sauce will keep for 2 to 3 days, covered with buttered wax paper, and refrigerated. The wax paper must touch the surface of the sauce.

32
Brown Mushroom Sauce

Yield: 2½ cups

This sauce is served with veal, steaks, filet, fondue bourguignon.

---

2   TABLESPOONS BUTTER
½   POUND MUSHROOMS, WASHED AND SLICED
2   DRIED SHALLOTS, FINELY CHOPPED
     SALT
     FRESHLY GROUND PEPPER
I   CUP DRY WHITE WINE
2½ CUPS HOT BASIC BROWN SAUCE THIN [*Recipe 28*]
½   TEASPOON TOMATO PASTE
I   PINCH TARRAGON
I   PINCH THYME
I   PINCH CHERVIL
3   TABLESPOONS HEAVY CREAM [OPTIONAL]
I   TABLESPOON FRESH PARSLEY, FINELY CHOPPED

In a heavy, medium size saucepan, melt the butter over high heat until it begins to foam. Reduce the heat to medium-high, add the mushrooms and the shallots, and sauté, uncovered, for 5 minutes, stirring frequently.

Season the mushrooms with salt and pepper.

Add the white wine, bring the liquid to a boil, and reduce the liquid by two-thirds.

Add the brown sauce, the tomato paste and the spices, and correct the seasonings, if necessary.

Bring the sauce to a boil over high heat, reduce the heat to low, and simmer, uncovered, for 30 minutes, stirring occasionally.

Mix in the cream just before serving, and garnish with the chopped parsley.

Basic Tomato Sauce

33
Quick Tomato Sauce

Yield: 2 cups

Serve this sauce with veal, casserole dishes, stuffed crêpes and pasta.

---

2   TABLESPOONS BUTTER
1   SMALL ONION, CUBED
1   SMALL CARROT, CUBED
½   STALK CELERY, CUBED
2   TABLESPOONS FLOUR
1   28 OUNCE CAN TOMATOES, DRAINED AND
      COARSELY CHOPPED
1   CUP HOT BASIC BROWN SAUCE THIN [*Recipe 28*]
1   TABLESPOON SUGAR
      BOUQUET GARNI CONSISTING OF
      PINCH OF THYME
1   BAY LEAF
¼   TEASPOON OREGANO
½   TEASPOON CHERVIL
1   GARLIC CLOVE, SMASHED AND FINELY CHOPPED
      FRESH PARSLEY
      CELERY [SEE BASIC BROWN BEEF STOCK 2, *Recipe 16*]
½   TEASPOON TOMATO PASTE
1   SMALL PINCH CAYENNE PEPPER
      SALT
      FRESHLY GROUND PEPPER

In a saucepan, melt the butter over high heat until it begins to foam. Reduce the heat to medium, add the onions, carrots and celery, and cook the vegetables, uncovered, for 5 minutes, stirring occasionally.

Add the flour to the vegetables, and cook the "roux", uncovered, for 3 minutes, stirring constantly.

Mix in the tomatoes, the brown sauce, the sugar, the bouquet garni and the tomato paste, and season the sauce with the cayenne pepper, salt and pepper.

Bring the sauce to a boil over high heat, reduce the heat to medium, and simmer the sauce, uncovered, for 45 minutes, stirring occasionally.
Strain.
If the sauce is too thick, dilute it with a bit of stock.

This sauce will keep for 2 to 3 days, covered with buttered wax paper and refrigerated. The wax paper must touch the surface of the sauce.

Egg Sauces

34
Béarnaise Sauce
Yield: ¾ cup

This sauce is served with steaks, brochettes, salmon steak, scallops, fondue bourguignon, eggs, chops, etc.

2	DRIED SHALLOTS, FINELY CHOPPED
10	PEPPERCORNS, COARSELY SMASHED
3	TABLESPOONS DRY WHITE WINE
1	TEASPOON TARRAGON
2	TABLESPOONS WINE VINEGAR
2	EGG YOLKS
1	TABLESPOON COLD WATER
¾	CUP MELTED CLARIFIED BUTTER

SALT

FRESHLY GROUND PEPPER

DASH OF CAYENNE PEPPER

1 TABLESPOON FRESH PARSLEY, FINELY CHOPPED

LEMON JUICE TO TASTE

In a stainless steel bowl, or in the top part of a double boiler, combine the shallots, peppercorns, white wine, tarragon and wine vinegar, and cook over medium heat, directly on top of the stove, until all the liquid has evaporated. Remove from the stove and let cool for a few minutes.

Blend in the egg yolks and the water with a whisk.

Place on top of a saucepan half-filled with almost boiling water and whisk constantly until thick.

When the sauce has thickened, add the clarified butter in a fine stream, whisking constantly.

Season the béarnaise with salt, pepper and cayenne pepper.

Strain the sauce and add the chopped parsley and lemon juice. Cover the sauce with buttered wax paper.

This sauce will keep, on top of the double boiler, over very low heat, for a maximum of 2 hours.

35
Hollandaise Sauce
Yield: ¾ cup

This sauce is served with fish and vegetables and used to gratiné fish and eggs.

2 EGG YOLKS

2 TABLESPOONS COLD WATER

¾ CUP MELTED CLARIFIED BUTTER

SALT
FRESHLY GROUND WHITE PEPPER
JUICE OF ¼ LEMON

Place the egg yolks in a stainless steel bowl or in the top part of a double boiler. Blend in 2 tablespoons water with a whisk. Place on top of a saucepan half-filled with almost boiling water and whisk until thick.

When the mixture has thickened, add the clarified butter in a fine stream, whisking constantly.

Season the hollandaise sauce with salt and pepper and blend in the lemon juice.

Cover the sauce with buttered wax paper.

This sauce will keep, on top of the double boiler, over very low heat, for a maximum of 2 hours.

36
Mousseline Sauce

Serve this sauce with asparagus, broccoli and use to glaze fish.

¾ CUP HOLLANDAISE SAUCE [*Recipe 35*]
4 TABLESPOONS HEAVY CREAM, WHIPPED VERY STIFF

Gently fold the whipped cream into the Hollandaise.

Cold Sauces

37
French Dressing, or Vinaigrette

For 4 people

Serve this vinaigrette with salads and cold vegetable hors d'oeuvre.

¼ TEASPOON SALT
   FRESHLY GROUND PEPPER TO TASTE
1 TEASPOON FRENCH DIJON MUSTARD
1 TABLESPOON DRIED SHALLOT, FINELY CHOPPED
1 TEASPOON FRESH PARSLEY, FINELY CHOPPED
3 TABLESPOONS WINE VINEGAR
7 TO 9 TABLESPOONS OLIVE OIL
   JUICE OF ¼ LEMON

In a mixing bowl, combine all the ingredients, except the olive oil and the lemon juice, with a whisk.

Add the olive oil in a thin stream, whisking constantly.

Add the lemon juice, blend well; correct the seasonings.

This dressing will keep for 2 to 3 weeks, refrigerated and covered.

Shake well before using.

38
French Dressing with Garlic

For 4 people

Serve this dressing with salads, and cold vegetable hors d'oeuvre.

¼ TEASPOON SALT
   FRESHLY GROUND PEPPER TO TASTE
1 TEASPOON FRENCH DIJON MUSTARD
1 TABLESPOON DRIED SHALLOT, FINELY CHOPPED
1 TEASPOON FRESH PARSLEY, FINELY CHOPPED
3 TABLESPOONS WINE VINEGAR
2 GARLIC CLOVES, SMASHED AND FINELY CHOPPED
7 TO 9 TABLESPOONS OLIVE OIL
   JUICE OF ¼ LEMON

In a mixing bowl, combine all the ingredients, except the olive oil and the lemon juice, with a whisk.

Add the olive oil in a thin stream, whisking constantly.

Add the lemon juice, blend well; correct the seasonings.

This dressing will keep for 2 to 3 weeks, covered and refrigerated.

Shake the dressing well before using.

39
French Dressing with Ailloli

For 4 people

Serve this dressing with salads, cold vegetable hors d'oeuvre and cold poached fish.

¾ CUP FRENCH DRESSING [*Recipe 37*]
2   TABLESPOONS AILLOLI SAUCE [*Recipe 49*]

Whisk 2 tablespoons ailloli sauce into the French Dressing.

40
Roquefort Dressing
Yield: 1¼ cups

This dressing is used for salads and cold green vegetable hors d'oeuvre.

¼ POUND ROQUEFORT CHEESE, SOFT AND
       MASHED
¼ TEASPOON SALT
     FRESHLY GROUND PEPPER TO TASTE
1   TEASPOON FRENCH DIJON MUSTARD
1   TABLESPOON DRIED SHALLOT, FINELY CHOPPED
1   TEASPOON FRESH PARSLEY, FINELY CHOPPED
3   TABLESPOONS WINE VINEGAR
7   TABLESPOONS OLIVE OIL
     JUICE OF ¼ LEMON
2   TABLESPOONS HEAVY CREAM
2   DROPS TABASCO SAUCE

In a mixing bowl, blend the salt, pepper, Dijon mustard, dry shallots, parsley and wine together with s whisk.

Add the olive oil in a thin stream, whisking constantly.

Blend in the lemon juice, the roquefort cheese and the cream, with a whisk.

Correct the seasonings.

41
Mayonnaise

Yield: 1 cup

---

2   EGG YOLKS
1   TEASPOON FRENCH DIJON MUSTARD OR
        ½ TEASPOON POWDERED ENGLISH MUSTARD
¾ CUPS VEGETABLE OR OLIVE OIL
1   TEASPOON WINE VINEGAR
    SALT
    FRESHLY GROUND WHITE PEPPER
    LEMON JUICE TO TASTE

In a small mixing bowl, whisk the egg yolks and mustard together until thick.

Add the oil, drop by drop, whisking constantly.
As soon as the mixture becomes thick, the flow of oil can be increased.

Incorporate the wine vinegar, salt and pepper to taste and the lemon juice.

In order to keep the mayonnaise for 5 to 6 days, mix in 1 teaspoon of hot water, cover with buttered wax paper and refrigerate. The hot water will prevent the mayonnaise from separating.

42
Green Mayonnaise

Add 1 tablespoon fresh parsley, finely chopped, to one cup of mayonnaise (Recipe 41) before serving.

43
Plum Sauce, Chinese Style

Yield: 2 cups

---

1 CUP CHINESE PLUM SAUCE*
1 CUP WHITE VINEGAR
FEW DROPS LEMON JUICE
SUGAR [OPTIONAL]

In a mixing bowl, combine all the ingredients together.

Serve the plum sauce with butterfly shrimp, egg rolls, etc.

*This plum sauce can be obtained in stores that carry the canned and dried chinese cooking ingredients. It is sold in one pound cans.

Shrimp

① peel shrimp

② remove ridge on top
with sharp knife...
de-vein

head

tail

... rinse in cold water

Cold Hors d'Oeuvre

44
Shrimp on Toast

For 6 to 8 people

½ POUND COOKED SHRIMP, PEELED, DEVEINED AND
    FINELY CHOPPED
      [SIZE: 15 TO 20 SHRIMP PER POUND, OR 21
        TO 25 SHRIMP PER POUND]   [*Recipe 111*]
3 TABLESPOONS MAYONNAISE [*Recipe 41*]
1 TABLESPOON FRESH PARSLEY, FINELY CHOPPED
1 TEASPOON FRESH CHIVES, FINELY CHOPPED
    SALT
    FRESHLY GROUND PEPPER
1 TEASPOON CURRY POWDER OR CURRY POWDER TO
    TASTE
    JUICE OF ¼ LEMON
2 DROPS TABASCO SAUCE

In a mixing bowl, blend all the ingredients thoroughly.

Correct the seasonings, if necessary.

If you wish to prepare the shrimp mixture ahead of time, it will keep for 6 to 7 hours, covered with buttered wax paper and refrigerated.

To serve, spread the shrimp mixture on toasted French bread which you have cut into various shapes, on melba toast or on crackers.

The canapés will keep for one hour.

45
Cocktail Mushroom Caps
For 6 to 10 people

---

4 CUPS MEDIUM SIZE MUSHROOM CAPS
½ CUP WATER
½ CUP DRY WHITE WINE
¼ CUP OLIVE OIL
2 TABLESPOONS WINE VINEGAR

BOUQUET GARNI CONSISTING OF
¼ TEASPOON THYME
2 BAY LEAVES
¼ TEASPOON FENNEL SEEDS
I TEASPOON CHERVIL
FRESH PARSLEY
CELERY [SEE BASIC BROWN BEEF STOCK 2, *Recipe 16*]
SALT
FRESHLY GROUND PEPPER

Combine all the ingredients in a medium size saucepan.

Cover, bring the liquid to a boil and then simmer the mushrooms over medium heat, for 8 minutes.

Let the mushrooms cool and refrigerate the mushrooms, in the marinade, for at least 12 hours.

The mushrooms will keep, refrigerated, for 48 hours, in the marinade.

Drain and discard the bouquet garni.

Serve with toothpicks.

46
Vegetables à la Grecque
For 6 to 10 people

---

2   CUPS RAW VEGETABLES*
½   CUP WATER
½   CUP DRY WHITE WINE
¼   CUP OLIVE OIL
2   TABLESPOONS WINE VINEGAR

BOUQUET GARNI CONSISTING OF
    ¼   TEASPOON THYME
    2   BAY LEAVES
    I   TEASPOON FENNEL SEEDS
    I   TEASPOON CHERVIL
        FRESH PARSLEY
        CELERY [SEE BASIC BROWN BEEF STOCK 2, *Recipe 16*]

    SALT
    FRESHLY GROUND PEPPER

Drop the vegetables into a large saucepan filled with boiling, salted water.

Cover the saucepan and blanch the vegetables for 5 to 6 minutes.

Remove the saucepan from the heat and cool the vegetables under running water for at least 4 minutes.

Drain the vegetables.

Combine all the ingredients, including the vegetables, in a medium size saucepan.

Cover, bring the liquid to a boil and then simmer the vegetables over medium heat, for 8 minutes.

Let the vegetables cool in the liquid and refrigerate the vegetables, in this marinade, for at least 12 hours.

The vegetables will keep, refrigerated, for 48 hours, in the marinade.

Drain and discard the bouquet garni.

Serve with toothpicks.

*Vegetables that can be used:
Cauliflower, florets
Green beans, cut into 1" strips
Broccoli, cut into 1" pieces
Carrots, cut into 1" strips
Zucchini, cut into 1" strips

47
Roquefort or Blue Cheese Canapés

For 6 to 8 people

½ POUND MASHED ROQUEFORT OR BLUE CHEESE AT
ROOM TEMPERATURE
5 TABLESPOONS UNSALTED BUTTER AT ROOM
TEMPERATURE
DROP OF TABASCO SAUCE
DASH OF PAPRIKA
DASH OF WORCESTERSHIRE SAUCE
COGNAC TO TASTE

In a mixing bowl, combine all the ingredients.

Spread the mixture on melba toast.

These canapés will keep for one hour.

48
Smoked Salmon Canapés

For 6 to 8 people

Smoked salmon should be rubbed lightly with oil when refrigerated, to prevent it from drying.

---

15 THIN SLICES SMOKED SALMON, CUT AT AN ANGLE
15 PIECES MELBA TOAST OR TOASTED FRENCH BREAD
½ POUND CREAM CHEESE AT ROOM TEMPERATURE
15 VERY THIN SLICES DRIED SHALLOT
1 TABLESPOON CAPERS
FEW LEMON WEDGES
FRESHLY GROUND PEPPER

Spread the cream cheese on the melba toast or French bread.

Cover with a slice of salmon.

Top with a slice of dried shallot and a few capers.

Arrange the canapés on a platter and decorate with lemon wedges.

Top with freshly ground pepper.

49
Ailloli on Toast *(Garlic Dip)*

For 6 to 8 people

This sauce is very popular in the South of France.
You can serve this sauce cold, with a poached fish such as halibut.

---

4 GARLIC CLOVES, SMASHED AND FINELY CHOPPED
2 EGG YOLKS
¾ CUP OLIVE OIL
SALT
FRESHLY GROUND PEPPER
LEMON JUICE TO TASTE
DASH OF CAYENNE PEPPER, OR A DROP OF TABASCO
SAUCE
MELBA TOAST OR TOASTED FRENCH BREAD

In a mortar, or in a small mixing bowl, thoroughly blend together the garlic and egg yolks with a whisk, until the mixture is thick.

Add the oil, drop by drop, whisking constantly.

Add the salt, pepper, lemon juice and cayenne pepper (or tabasco sauce); and correct seasonings, if necessary.

Your guests will spread the ailloli on melba toast or toasted French bread.

You can prepare the ailloli ahead of time. It should be covered with buttered wax paper and refrigerated.

Hot Hors d'Oeuvres

50
Croque Monsieur

For 6 to 8 people

16	THIN SLICES FRENCH BREAD
8	SLICES GRUYÈRE OR MOZZARELLA CHEESE
8	THIN SLICES VERY LEAN HAM
	CAYENNE PEPPER
1½	TABLESPOONS CLARIFIED BUTTER

Remove the crusts from the French bread.

Place a slice of cheese and a slice of ham on a slice of French bread and add a dash of cayenne pepper.

Cover with another slice of bread and butter the outside of the croque-monsieur.

In a sauté pan, melt 1½ tablespoons clarified butter.

Brown the croque-monsieur on both sides, in the melted butter.

Cut into triangles and serve immediately.

51
Water Chestnuts à la Diable

For 6 to 8 people

---

4 OUNCE CAN WHOLE WATER CHESTNUTS, DRAINED
    AND CUT IN TWO
8 TO 10 SLICES BACON, CUT IN HALF
    CAYENNE PEPPER

Preheat the oven to "broil".

Wrap the water chestnuts in the bacon.

Secure the bacon with a toothpick and place the water chestnuts on a rack, in a roasting pan.

Broil for 3 to 4 minutes on each side, 4 inches away from the upper broiling element.

Remove the water chestnuts from the roasting pan and drain them on paper towels.

Sprinkle with cayenne pepper and serve immediately.

52
Butterfly Shrimp

For 6 to 8 people

---

1 POUND OF RAW SHRIMP, IN THEIR SHELL
   [SIZE 15 TO 20 SHRIMPS PER POUND]
2 GARLIC CLOVES, SMASHED AND FINELY CHOPPED
   JUICE OF 1 LEMON
   SALT
   FRESHLY GROUND PEPPER
   PEANUT OIL
   BASIC BATTER FOR DEEP-FRYING [*Recipe 4*]

Peel each shrimp down to the last section, leaving it and the tail attached to the shrimp. Devein and wash the shrimp. Cut each shrimp ¾ of the way through along its inner curve. Flatten the shrimp with the palm of your hand.

In a mixing bowl, combine all the ingredients except the peanut oil. Cover the shrimp with wax paper and set aside.

While the shrimp are marinating, prepare batter.

Half fill a deep fryer with peanut oil and heat the oil to 350°.

Dip the shrimp, one at a time, into the batter and then drop them carefully into the hot oil.

Deep fry the shrimp for 3 to 4 minutes, or until golden brown.

Drain the shrimp on paper towels and serve them with Plum Sauce (Recipe 43).

53
Mushroom Caps
Stuffed with Crab Meat

For 6 to 8 people

---

24 LARGE MUSHROOM CAPS [1½" IN DIAMETER]
2 TABLESPOONS BUTTER
2 DRIED SHALLOTS, FINELY CHOPPED
½ POUND CRAB MEAT [FRESH OR CANNED AND
    DRAINED] COARSELY CHOPPED
    SALT
    FRESHLY GROUND PEPPER
    FEW DROPS OF TABASCO SAUCE
½ CUP HOT WHITE SAUCE THICK [*Recipe 25*]
½ CUP GRATED SWISS OR MOZZARELLA CHEESE

Preheat the oven to 350°.

In a heavy, medium size saucepan, melt the butter over high heat, until it begins to foam.
Reduce the heat to medium, add the dry shallots and cook the shallots, uncovered, for 3 minutes.

Mix in the crab meat and season with salt, pepper and a few drops of tabasco sauce.

Cook the mixture over low heat, uncovered, for 4 minutes.
Stir the white sauce into the mixture; season well.

Arrange the mushroom caps in an oiled baking dish.
Season the mushroom caps with salt and pepper and fill them with the crab meat mixture.
Sprinkle the mushrooms with the grated cheese.

Bake the mushrooms in the oven for 15 minutes.
Serve immediately on individual plates.

54
Mushroom Caps
Stuffed with Spinach and Ham
For 6 to 8 people

---

24 LARGE MUSHROOM CAPS [1½" IN DIAMETER]
 1 CUP COOKED SPINACH* FINELY CHOPPED
 2 TABLESPOONS BUTTER
 3 DRIED SHALLOTS FINELY CHOPPED
¼ CUP HAM FINELY DICED
½ CUP HOT THICK WHITE SAUCE [*Recipe 25*]
   SALT
   FRESHLY GROUND PEPPER
   DROP OF TABASCO SAUCE
   DROP OF WORCESTERSHIRE SAUCE
   BREADCRUMBS

Preheat the oven to 350°.

In a heavy, medium size saucepan, melt the butter over high heat, until it begins to foam.

Reduce the heat to medium, add the dry shallots and cook the shallots, uncovered, for 3 minutes, stirring frequently.

Add the Spinach and the ham to the shallots and cook the mixture, uncovered, for 3 to 4 minutes, stirring frequently.

Stir the white sauce into the mixture and season with salt, pepper, tabasco sauce and worcestershire sauce.

Arrange the mushroom caps in an oiled baking dish.
Season the mushroom caps with salt and pepper and fill them with the spinach-ham mixture.
Sprinkle the mushroom caps with breadcrumbs.

Bake the mushrooms in the oven for 15 minutes.

Serve the mushroom caps immediately on individual plates.

*Parboil the spinach for 6 minutes, in boiling salted water.
Cool the spinach for 4 minutes under running water.

Remove all moisture from the spinach by forming the spinach into a ball and squeezing it in the palms of your hand.

Cold Entrées

55
Halibut Served on Lettuce Hearts

For 4 people

1	POUND HALIBUT
	SALT
	FRESHLY GROUND PEPPER
1	PINCH THYME
1	BAY LEAF
1	TEASPOON CHERVIL
5	MUSHROOMS, SLICED
½	CUP WHITE WINE OR 2 TABLESPOONS WINE VINEGAR
	JUICE OF ¼ LEMON
12	GREEN OLIVES, PITTED AND SLICED
5	WATER CHESTNUTS, THINLY SLICED
½	CUP FRENCH DRESSING [*Recipe 37*]
4	LETTUCE HEARTS
1	HARD BOILED EGG, CUT INTO 4 PIECES
4	LEMON WEDGES
	FRESH PARSLEY

Wash the halibut under cold running water.

Place the halibut in a buttered pan, season with salt and pepper, and add the thyme, bay leaf, chervil, mushrooms, wine or wine vinegar, lemon juice and cold water to cover.

Cover the pan with buttered wax paper. Press the wax paper down with your fingertips so that it touches the surface of the ingredients.

Bring the liquid to a boil over high heat, on top of the stove.
Reduce the heat to low and simmer for 15 minutes.
Remove the pan from the heat and let the halibut cool in the liquid.

Remove the halibut from the pan and flake into a mixing bowl.
Mix in the sliced olives, water chestnuts and the French dressing.
Correct the seasonings.

Arrange the halibut on the lettuce hearts.
Decorate with the hard boiled egg, the lemon wedges and the parsley.

56
Scampi
Served in a Scallop Shell

For 4 people

20	UNCOOKED SCAMPI IN THE SHELL
	[SIZE 18 TO 24 SCAMPI PER POUND]
1½	CUPS WATER
	SALT
	FRESHLY GROUND PEPPER
1	TEASPOON WHITE VINEGAR
½	CUP MAYONNAISE [*Recipe 41*]
1	TEASPOON CURRY POWDER
	JUICE OF ¼ LEMON
1	TEASPOON FRESH PARSLEY, FINELY CHOPPED
4	LEMON WEDGES

In a medium size saucepan, bring the cold water, salt, vinegar and scampi to a boil, over high heat.

Remove the saucepan from the heat and cool the scampi under running water for at least 4 minutes.

With a pair of kitchen scissors, cut the inner shells of the scampi and remove the scampi from the shell.

In a mixing bowl, combine the scampi, mayonnaise, curry powder, lemon juice and parsley.

Correct the seasonings.

Spoon the mixture into the individual scallop shells and garnish with a lemon wedge.

57
Avocado à la Martin

For 2 people

---

1 AVOCADO
5 OR 6 COOKED SHRIMP, PEELED AND DEVEINED
    [SIZE 15 TO 20 SHRIMPS PER POUND]
3 OR 4 WALNUTS, COARSELY CHOPPED
3 TABLESPOONS MAYONNAISE [*Recipe 41*]
    SALT
    FRESHLY GROUND PEPPER
    FEW DROPS OF TABASCO SAUCE
1 TEASPOON FRESH PARSLEY, FINELY CHOPPED

With a spoon, scoop out the flesh of the avocado.

Cut the shrimp in two, at an angle.

Mix all the ingredients together, including the avocado flesh. Spoon the mixture into the avocado shells.

58
Garden Cantaloupe
For 2 people

---

1 CANTALOUPE
½ CUP PORT WINE OR SHERRY
2 CUPS CRUSHED ICE

Cut the cantaloupe in two and remove the seeds.

Scoop out the flesh of the cantaloupe with a melon baller.

Replace the flesh in the cantaloupe shells.
Pour 2 ounces port wine or sherry into each cantaloupe shell.

Cover the cantaloupe with wax paper and refrigerate for 3 hours.

Serve in a bowl, surrounded by crushed ice.

Hot Entrées

59
Snails Provençale
For 2 people

¼ POUND GARLIC BUTTER AT ROOM TEMPERATURE
[RECIPE 8]
12 LARGE CANNED SNAILS, DRAINED
12 SNAIL SHELLS

Preheat the oven to Broil.

Spoon ¼ teaspoon of garlic butter inside each shell.

Put the snails in the shells and seal the shells with the remaining garlic butter.

Arrange the shells in snail dishes.

Broil the snails, 4" away from the upper broiling element, for 8 to 10 minutes.

The snails are ready when the butter is golden brown.

60
Snails au Gratin

For 2 people

½   POUND GARLIC BUTTER AT ROOM TEMPERATURE
     [RECIPE 8]
12   LARGE CANNED SNAILS, DRAINED
 3   TABLESPOONS GRATED GRUYÈRE CHEESE
     DASH OF CAYENNE PEPPER
 2   OVENPROOF CERAMIC SNAIL DISHES

Preheat the oven to Broil.

Spoon ¼ teaspoon of garlic butter inside each slot of the snail dishes.

Drop a snail in each slot, on top of the butter.

Cover the snails with the remaining garlic butter.

Sprinkle the snails with the grated cheese and season with a dash of cayenne pepper.

Bake the snails, in the middle of the oven, for 15 minutes.

61
Snails Bouguignon

For 2 people

12	LARGE CANNED SNAILS DRAINED
2	TABLESPOONS BUTTER
12	MUSHROOMS QUARTERED
2	DRIED SHALLOTS FINELY CHOPPED
20	CROUTONS
	SALT
	FRESHLY GROUND PEPPER
½	CUP HOT BOURGUIGNON SAUCE [*Recipe 30*]
1	TABLESPOON FRESH PARSLEY FINELY CHOPPED

In a small sauté pan, melt the butter over high heat, until it begins to foam. Add the mushrooms and sauté for 5 minutes, stirring frequently.

Reduce the heat to medium, add the shallots, the croutons and the snails to the mushrooms; cook the mixture, uncovered, for 2 minutes, stirring occasionally.

Add the sauce to the mixture and simmer, uncovered, for 2 minutes.

Season to taste and garnish with the chopped parsley.

Serve the Snails Bourguignon in a Coquille St.Jacques shell.

62
Crêpes Stuffed with Shrimp
For 4 people

---

4   CRÊPES [*Recipe 5*]
1   POUND COOKED SHRIMP, PEELED AND DEVEINED
    [RECIPE 111]
2   TABLESPOONS BUTTER
2   TABLESPOONS DRY SHALLOTS, FINELY CHOPPED
    PAPRIKA TO TASTE
½   CUP PORT WINE
1½ CUPS HOT WHITE SAUCE THICK [*Recipe 25*]
½   CUP GRATED GRUYÈRE OR MOZZARELLA CHEESE
1   TABLESPOON CHOPPED PARSLEY
    SALT
    FRESHLY GROUND PEPPER

Preheat the oven to 350°.

Slice the shrimp diagonally.

In a sauté pan, melt the butter over high heat, until it begins to foam. Reduce the heat to medium and add the shallots and the shrimp. Cook this mixture, uncovered, for 3 minutes, stirring occasionally.

Mix in the paprika to taste and pour in the port wine. Increase the heat to high, and cook the mixture, uncovered, for 2 to 3 minutes.

Mix in the white sauce, season the mixture to taste and remove the pan from the heat.

Separate the mixture in two and reserve one half of the mixture.

Stuff the crêpes with one half of the mixture and roll the edges of the crêpes over the mixture.
Arrange the crêpes in a buttered baking dish, rolled edge down

and pour the remaining half of the shrimp mixture on top of the crêpes.

Sprinkle the crêpes with grated cheese.

Turn on the broiling element of the oven and bake the crêpes, in the middle of the oven, for 15 minutes.

Before serving, sprinkle the crêpes with chopped parsley.

63
Coquilles St-Jacques

For 4 people

1	POUND RAW SCALLOPS
2	DRIED SHALLOTS, FINELY CHOPPED
1/4	CUP DRY WHITE WINE
1/4	CUP WATER
	SALT
	FRESHLY GROUND WHITE PEPPER
1	CUP HOT WHITE SAUCE THICK [*Recipe 25*]
	DASH OF CAYENNE PEPPER
2	TABLESPOONS THIN CREAM
1/4	CUP GRATED GRUYÈRE CHEESE

Preheat the oven to Broil.

In a sauté pan, combine the scallops, the shallots, the white wine, the water, salt and pepper to taste and cover with buttered foil or wax paper. Gently press the paper down with your fingertips so that the paper touches the surface of the ingredients.

Bring the liquid to a boil over high heat.

Reduce the heat to medium and simmer the scallops for 5 minutes.

Remove the scallops from the liquid and put them aside in a heated platter.

Reduce the remaining liquid in the sauté pan by two-thirds over high heat.

Reduce the heat to medium, blend in the white sauce, season with salt, pepper and cayenne pepper; simmer, uncovered, for 8 to 10 minutes.

Add the scallops and the thin cream to the sauce; pour the mixture into four coquille St-Jacques shells.

Sprinkle each coquille with the grated cheese; bake, 6" to 8" away from the upper broiling element, for 8 to 10 minutes.

64
Brochettes of Scampi
For 4 people

---

24 UNCOOKED SCAMPI IN THE SHELL
　　[SIZE 18 TO 24 SCAMPI PER POUND]
24 MUSHROOM CAPS
　4 TO 5 SLICES BACON CUT INTO 1" SQUARES
　4 TABLESPOONS GARLIC BUTTER AT ROOM
　　TEMPERATURE [*Recipe 8*]
　　SALT
　　FRESHLY GROUND PEPPER
　　JUICE OF 1 LEMON

Preheat the oven to Broil.

Remove the scampi from the shell.

On a skewer, alternate the scampi, mushroom caps and bacon.

Season the brochettes in a baking dish and dot with garlic butter.

Bake the brochettes, 6" away from the broiling element, for 3 minutes on each side.

Before serving, squeeze the lemon juice onto the brochettes.

65
Baked Oysters au Gratin
For 4 people

---

24 FRESH OYSTERS IN THE SHELL
2½ CUPS HOT WHITE SAUCE THICK [*Recipe 25*]
DASH OF CAYENNE PEPPER
1 TABLESPOON MELTED BUTTER
½ CUP GRATED PARMESAN CHEESE
4 TABLESPOONS BUTTER

Preheat the oven to broil.

Remove the oysters from the shell and reserve the liquid from the oysters.

Thoroughly clean 24 oyster shells.

Season the white sauce with cayenne pepper; mix in 1 tablespoon melted butter and the reserved juice from the oysters.

Arrange the shells in a baking dish.

Spoon 1 tablespoon white sauce into each oyster shell.

Place an oyster into each shell.

Spoon the remaining white sauce over the oysters and sprinkle with grated cheese.

Dot the shells with butter.

Bake the oysters, 4" away from the broiling element, for 3 to 4 minutes.

66
Mussels à la Crème
For 4 people

---

5 POUNDS FRESH MUSSELS IN THE SHELL,
   WELL WASHED AND SCRUBBED
3 TABLESPOONS BUTTER
2 TABLESPOONS DRY SHALLOTS, FINELY CHOPPED
1 CUP DRY WHITE WINE
  SALT
  FRESHLY GROUND PEPPER
1 PINCH THYME
½ TEASPOON CHERVIL
1 CUP HEAVY CREAM
1 TEASPOON FRESH PARSLEY, FINELY CHOPPED
2 TABLESPOONS KNEADED BUTTER [MANIÉ BUTTER]
   [*Recipe 12*]

Place the mussels, butter, chopped shallots, white wine, salt, pepper, thyme and chervil in a large pot.

Cover the pot, and cook the mussels over high heat, until the shells open.

Remove the mussels from the pot and reserve the liquid.

In a small saucepan, combine the cooking liquid, the heavy cream and the parsley. Reduce the liquid, over high heat, for 6 to 8 minutes, and correct the seasonings.

Remove the mussels from the shells and arrange them on a heated platter.

Thicken the sauce with kneaded butter and pour the sauce over the mussels.

Cream Soups
THICKENED WITH FLOUR

67
Cream of Asparagus Soup
For 4 people

---

1 BUNCH FRESH ASPARAGUS, COOKED* OR
   1-14 OUNCE CAN ASPARAGUS, DRAINED, OR
   10 OUNCES FROZEN ASPARAGUS, COOKED*, AND
   COARSELY CHOPPED
3 TABLESPOONS ASPARAGUS TIPS RESERVED AS A
   GARNISH
6 TABLESPOONS BUTTER
1 SMALL ONION THINLY SLICED
5 TABLESPOONS FLOUR
6 CUPS HOT BASIC CHICKEN STOCK
   [*Recipe 17 or 18*] OR
   6 CUPS HOT ASPARAGUS STOCK
   SALT
   FRESHLY GROUND PEPPER

BOUQUET GARNI CONSISTING OF
   ¼ TEASPOON THYME
   1 BAY LEAF
   ½ TEASPOON CHERVIL
   ¼ TEASPOON BASIL
   1 WHOLE CLOVE
   FRESH PARSLEY
   CELERY [SEE BASIC BROWN BEEF STOCK *Recipe 16*]
2 TABLESPOONS HEAVY CREAM [OPTIONAL]
1 TABLESPOON FRESH PARSLEY, FINELY CHOPPED OR
   1 TABLESPOON FRESH CHIVES, FINELY CHOPPED

In a heavy, medium size saucepan, melt 5 tablespoons butter over high heat until it begins to foam. Reduce the heat to low and add the sliced onion. Cover and simmer the onion for a few minutes.

Add the chopped asparagus to the onions, cover and simmer for 15 minutes, stirring occasionally.

Add the flour to the vegetables and cook, uncovered, for 3 minutes, stirring constantly.

Remove the saucepan from the heat, add one cup of stock and mix in thoroughly with a wooden spoon. Return the saucepan to the heat and add the remaining stock, one cup at a time, until desired consistency is reached, stirring constantly.

Season the soup to taste and add the bouquet garni.
Bring the liquid to a boil, reduce the heat to low and simmer, uncovered, for 40 minutes, stirring occasionally.

Correct the seasonings and strain the soup.

If the soup is too thick, mix in a bit of hot stock with a wooden spoon.

In a small saucepan, simmer the reserved asparagus tips in 1 tablespoon butter, for 3 minutes.

Before serving the soup, mix in the cream and garnish with the asparagus tips and the chopped parsley (or chives).

This soup, without the cream, will keep for 2 to 3 days, refrigerated and covered with buttered wax paper.

If you wish to serve this soup chilled, add ¼ cup heavy cream, instead of 2 tablespoons heavy cream.

*Drop the asparagus into a large saucepan filled with boiling, salted water.

Cover and blanch the asparagus for 8 to 10 minutes.

Remove the saucepan from the heat, cool the asparagus under running water for at least 4 minutes and drain.

68
Cream of Mushroom Soup
For 4 people

¾ POUND FRESH MUSHROOMS FINELY SLICED OR
    1 - 14 OUNCE CAN MUSHROOMS DRAINED
    AND CHOPPED
4 TABLESPOONS MUSHROOMS FINELY CHOPPED,
    RESERVED AS A GARNISH
5 TABLESPOONS BUTTER
1 SMALL ONION THINLY SLICED
5 TABLESPOONS FLOUR
6 CUPS HOT BASIC CHICKEN STOCK
    [*Recipe 17 or 18*]
    SALT
    FRESHLY GROUND PEPPER

BOUQUET GARNI CONSISTING OF
    ¼ TEASPOON THYME
    1 BAY LEAF
    ½ TEASPOON CHERVIL
    ¼ TEASPOON BASIL
    1 WHOLE CLOVE
    FRESH PARSLEY
    CELERY [SEE BASIC BROWN BEEF STOCK 2, *Recipe 16*]
2 TABLESPOONS HEAVY CREAM [OPTIONAL]
1 TABLESPOON FRESH PARSLEY, FINELY CHOPPED OR
    1 TABLESPOON FRESH CHIVES, FINELY CHOPPED

In a heavy, medium size saucepan, melt the butter over high heat until it begins to foam. Reduce heat to low and add the sliced onion. Cover and simmer the onion for a few minutes.

Add the mushrooms to the onions, cover and simmer for 15 minutes, stirring occasionally.

Add the flour to the vegetables and cook, uncovered, for 3 minutes, stirring constantly.

Remove the saucepan from the heat, add one cup of stock and mix in thoroughly with a wooden spoon. Return the saucepan to the heat; add the remaining stock, one cup at a time, until desired consistency is reached, stirring constantly.

Season the soup to taste and add the bouquet garni.
Bring the liquid to a boil, reduce the heat to low and simmer, uncovered, for 40 minutes, stirring occasionally.

Correct the seasonings and strain the soup.

If the soup is too thick, mix in a bit of hot chicken stock with a wooden spoon.

In a small saucepan, simmer the reserved chopped mushrooms in $1/2$ cup chicken stock, for a few minutes.

Before serving the soup, mix in the cream and garnish with the reserved mushrooms and with the chopped parsley (or chives).

This soup, without the cream, will keep for 2 to 3 days, covered with buttered wax paper and refrigerated.

69
Cream of Cucumber Soup
For 4 people

I recommend that this soup be served chilled.

---

3 CUCUMBERS PEELED, SEEDED AND FINELY SLICED
½ CUCUMBER FINELY CHOPPED, RESERVED AS A
   GARNISH
6 TABLESPOONS BUTTER
1 SMALL ONION, THINLY SLICED
5 TABLESPOONS FLOUR
6 CUPS HOT BASIC CHICKEN STOCK
   [*Recipe 17 or 18*]
   SALT
   FRESHLY GROUND PEPPER

BOUQUET GARNI CONSISTING OF
   ¼ TEASPOON THYME
   1 BAY LEAF
   ½ TEASPOON CHERVIL
   ¼ TEASPOON BASIL
   1 WHOLE CLOVE
      FRESH PARSLEY
      CELERY [SEE BASIC BROWN BEEF STOCK 2,
        Recipe 16]
2 TABLESPOONS HEAVY CREAM [OPTIONAL]
1 TABLESPOON FRESH PARSLEY, FINELY CHOPPED OR
   1 TABLESPOON FRESH CHIVES, FINELY CHOPPED

In a heavy, medium size saucepan, melt 5 tablespoons butter over high heat until it begins to foam. Reduce the heat to low, and add the sliced onion. Cover and simmer the onion for a few minutes.

Add the sliced cucumbers to the onions, cover and simmer for 15 minutes, stirring occasionally.

Add the flour to the vegetables and cook, uncovered, for 3 minutes, stirring constantly.

Remove the saucepan from the heat, add one cup of stock and mix in thoroughly with a wooden spoon. Return the saucepan to the heat; add the remaining stock, one cup at a time, until desired consistency is reached, stirring constantly.

Season the soup to taste and add the bouquet garni.
Bring the liquid to a boil, reduce the heat to low and simmer, uncovered, for 40 minutes, stirring occasionally.

Correct the seasonings and strain the soup.

If the soup is too thick, mix in a bit of hot chicken stock with a wooden spoon.

In a small saucepan, melt 1 tablespoon butter over high heat, until it begins to foam. Reduce the heat to medium and add the reserved chopped cucumbers. Simmer the cucumber, uncovered, for a few minutes.

Before serving, mix in the cream and garnish with the chopped cucumber and parsley (or chives).

If you wish to serve this soup chilled, add ¼ cup heavy cream instead of 2 tablespoons heavy cream.

70
Cream of Tomato Soup
For 4 people

---

5 MEDIUM SIZE TOMATOES, COARSELY CHOPPED OR
    1 - 28 OUNCE CAN OF TOMATOES, DRAINED AND
    CHOPPED
5 TABLESPOONS BUTTER
1 SMALL ONION, THINLY SLICED
5 TABLESPOONS FLOUR
6 CUPS HOT BASIC CHICKEN STOCK [*Recipe 17 and 18*]
1 TEASPOON TOMATO PASTE [OPTIONAL]
1 TABLESPOON SUGAR
   SALT
   FRESHLY GROUND PEPPER

BOUQUET GARNI CONSISTING OF
¼ TEASPOON THYME
1 BAY LEAF
½ TEASPOON CHERVIL
¼ TEASPOON BASIL
¼ TEASPOON OREGANO
1 WHOLE CLOVE
   FRESH PARSLEY
   CELERY [SEE BASIC BROWN BEEF STOCK 2, *Recipe 16*]
2 TABLESPOONS HEAVY CREAM [OPTIONAL]
1 TABLESPOON FRESH PARSLEY FINELY CHOPPED OR
    1 TABLESPOON FRESH CHIVES FINELY CHOPPED

In a heavy, medium size saucepan, melt the butter over high heat until it begins to foam. Reduce the heat to low and add the sliced onion. Cover, and simmer the onion for a few minutes.

Add the chopped tomatoes to the onion, cover and simmer for 15 minutes, stirring occasionally.

Add the flour to the vegetables and cook, uncovered, for 3 minutes, stirring constantly.

Remove the saucepan from the heat, add one cup of stock, and mix in thoroughly with a wooden spoon. Return the saucepan to the heat; add the remaining stock, one cup at a time, until desired consistency is reached, while stirring constantly.

Add the tomato paste and the sugar, season to taste and add the bouquet garni.

Bring the liquid to a boil, reduce the heat to low and simmer, uncovered, for 40 minutes, stirring occasionally.

Correct the seasonings and strain the soup.

If the soup is too thick, mix in a bit of hot chicken stock with a wooden spoon.

Before serving, mix in the cream and garnish with the chopped parsley (or chives).

This soup, without the cream, will keep for 2 to 3 days, refrigerated and covered with buttered wax paper.

If you wish to serve this soup chilled, add ¼ cup heavy cream instead of 2 tablespoons heavy cream.

Cream Soups
THICKENED WITH POTATO

71
Parmentier Cream Soup
For 4 people

2 TABLESPOONS BUTTER
2 LEEKS, WHITE PART ONLY, THINLY SLICED
1 LARGE ONION, THINLY SLICED
1½ POUNDS OR 4 LARGE RAW POTATOES, PEELED AND
   THINLY SLICED
6 CUPS HOT BASIC CHICKEN STOCK [*Recipe 17 and 18*]

BOUQUET GARNI CONSISTING OF
¼ TEASPOON THYME
1 BAY LEAF
¼ TEASPOON BASIL
½ TEASPOON CHEVRIL
   FRESH PARSLEY
   CELERY [SEE BASIC BROWN BEEF STOCK 2, *Recipe 16*]

   SALT
   FRESHLY GROUND PEPPER
2 TABLESPOONS HEAVY CREAM

In a heavy, medium size saucepan, melt the butter over high heat until it begins to foam. Reduce the heat to low and add the sliced leeks and onion. Cover and simmer for 15 minutes, stirring occasionally.

Add the potatoes, enough chicken stock, until desired consistency is reached, and the bouquet garni to the leeks and onion; season to taste with salt and pepper.

Bring the liquid to a boil, over high heat, reduce the heat to medium, and simmer, uncovered, for 40 minutes, stirring occasionally.

Strain the soup and correct the seasonings.

If the soup is too thick, mix in a bit of hot chicken stock with a wooden spoon.

Before serving, mix in the cream.

This soup, without the cream, will keep for 2 to 3 days, refrigerated and covered with buttered wax paper.

72
Cream of Leek Soup
For 4 people

---

3 LEEKS, WHITE PART ONLY, THINLY SLICED

2 TABLESPOONS LEEK, THINLY SLICED, RESERVED AS
A GARNISH

2½ TABLESPOONS BUTTER

1 LARGE ONION, THINLY SLICED

1½ POUNDS OR 4 LARGE RAW POTATOES, PEELED AND
THINLY SLICED

6 CUPS HOT BASIC CHICKEN STOCK *(Recipe 17 or 18]*

BOUQUET GARNI CONSISTING OF
¼ TEASPOON THYME
1 BAY LEAF
¼ TEASPOON BASIL
½ TEASPOON CHERVIL
FRESH PARSLEY
CELERY [SEE BASIC BROWN BEEF STOCK 2, *Recipe 16]*

SALT
FRESHLY GROUND PEPPER
2 TABLESPOONS HEAVY CREAM

In a heavy, medium size saucepan, melt 2 tablespoons butter over high heat until it begins to foam. Reduce the heat to low and add the sliced leeks and onion. Cover, and simmer for 15 minutes, stirring occasionally.

Add the potatoes, enough chicken stock, until desired consistency is reached, to the leeks and onion; season to taste with salt and pepper.

Bring the liquid to a boil over high heat, reduce the heat to medium and simmer, uncovered, for 40 minutes, stirring occasionally.

Strain the soup, and correct the seasonings.

If the soup is too thick, mix in a bit of hot chicken stock with a wooden spoon.

In a small sauté pan, melt ½ tablespoon butter over high heat. Reduce the heat to medium, add the reserved 2 tablespoons of leek and simmer, uncovered, for 3 minutes, stirring occasionally.

Before serving, mix the cream into the soup and garnish with the leeks.

73
Cream of Carrot Soup
For 4 people

4 LARGE CARROTS, PEELED AND THINLY SLICED
4 SLICES BACON, DICED
1 LARGE ONION, THINLY SLICED
4 LARGE RAW POTATOES, PEELED AND THINLY SLICED
6 CUPS HOT BASIC CHICKEN STOCK
   [*Recipe 17 or 18*]

BOUQUET GARNI CONSISTING OF
    ¼ TEASPOON THYME
    1 BAY LEAF
    ¼ TEASPOON CHERVIL
    ¼ TEASPOON BASIL
    ½ TEASPOON CHERVIL
       FRESH PARSLEY
       CELERY [SEE BASIC BROWN BEEF STOCK 2, *Recipe 16*]

    SALT
    FRESHLY GROUND PEPPER
2 TABLESPOONS HEAVY CREAM

In a heavy, medium size saucepan, cook the bacon over medium heat, uncovered, for 5 minutes.

Add the sliced onion to the bacon, cover and simmer for a few minutes, stirring occasionally. Reduce the heat to low and add the sliced carrots; cover and simmer for 15 minutes, stirring occasionally.

Add the potatoes, enough stock until desired consistency is reached, and the bouquet garni to the onions and carrots. Season with salt and pepper and bring the liquid to a boil, over high heat. Reduce the heat to medium and simmer the soup, uncovered, for 40 minutes, stirring occasionally.
Correct the seasonings and rub the soup through a fine sieve. If the soup is too thick, mix in a bit of hot chicken stock.

Before serving, stir in the heavy cream.

This soup, without the cream, will keep for 2 to 3 days, covered with buttered wax paper and refrigerated.

Clear Soups

74
Vegetable Soup
For 4 people

- 1 TABLESPOON BUTTER
- ½ LEEK, THINLY SLICED
- 1 SMALL ONION, DICED
- 1 PINCH BASIL
- ½ TEASPOON CHERVIL
- 1 BAY LEAF
- 1 PINCH THYME
- ½ GREEN PEPPER, SEEDED AND DICED
- ½ CELERY STALK, DICED
- 1 SMALL CARROT, FINELY CHOPPED
- 1 MEDIUM SIZE RAW POTATO, PEELED AND DICED [OPTIONAL]
- 5 CUPS HOT BEEF, CHICKEN OR VEGETABLE STOCK [SEE *Stocks*]
  SALT
  FRESHLY GROUND PEPPER
  CROUTONS
- 1 TABLESPOON FRESH PARSELY, FINELY CHOPPED

In a heavy, medium size saucepan, melt the butter over high heat. Reduce the heat to low and add the leek and onion; cover and simmer for a few minutes.

Add the herbs, the remaining vegetables and the stock; season the soup to taste with salt and pepper.

Bring the soup to a boil over high heat.

Lower the heat to medium and simmer the soup, uncovered, until the vegetables are cooked.

Garnish the soup with the croutons and parsley.

75
Onion Soup au Gratin
For 4 people

---

 3 MEDIUM SIZE ONIONS, PEELED AND THINLY SLICED
 2 TABLESPOONS BUTTER
¼ CUP DRY WHITE WINE OR
   3 TABLESPOONS COGNAC
 2 TABLESPOONS FLOUR
 6 CUPS HOT BASIC BEEF STOCK
   [*Recipe 15 or 16*]
 1 BAY LEAF
   SALT
   FRESHLY GROUND PEPPER
   DROP OF TABASCO SAUCE
1½ CUPS GRATED GRUYÈRE CHEESE
 4 SLICES TOASTED FRENCH BREAD
 4 OVENPROOF EARTHENWARE ONION SOUP BOWLS

In a heavy, medium size saucepan, melt the butter over high heat until it begins to foam. Reduce the heat to very low and add the onions; simmer, uncovered, for 20 minutes, stirring occasionally (add a bit of butter during the cooking process, if necessary).

Increase the heat to high, pour the wine (or cognac) into the onions; reduce the liquid by two thirds.

Reduce the heat to medium and sprinkle the flour onto the onions.

Gradually mix in the beef stock, add the bay leaf and season to taste with salt and pepper.

Bring the liquid to a boil over high heat.
Reduce the heat to low and simmer the soup, uncovered, for 30 minutes, stirring occasionally.
Add a drop of tabasco sauce to the soup and correct the seasonings.

Remove the bay leaf from the soup.

Preheat the oven to Broil.
Place 1 tablespoon grated cheese in the bottom of each bowl.
Pour the soup into each bowl.

Cover the soup with a slice of toasted French bread and sprinkle the bread with the grated cheese.

Broil the soup, in the middle of the oven, for 15 to 20 minutes.

This soup will keep for 3 days, covered with buttered wax paper and refrigerated.

This soup will keep, frozen, for 3 months.

76
Clam Chowder
For 4 people

---

3 DOZEN FRESH CLAMS, REMOVED FROM THE SHELL
   AND COARSELY CHOPPED OR
   2 - 10 OUNCE CANS CLAMS, DRAINED
   RESERVE THE LIQUID FROM THE CLAMS
1 TABLESPOON BUTTER
1 MEDIUM SIZE ONION, PEELED AND DICED
1 GREEN PEPPER, SEEDED AND DICED
2 SMALL RAW POTATOES, PEELED AND DICED
2½ CUPS HOT BASIC FISH STOCK [*Recipe 19*]
1 PINCH THYME
1 BAY LEAF
1 TEASPOON FRESH PARSLEY, FINELY CHOPPED
¼ TEASPOON CHERVIL
1 PINCH TARRAGON
   SALT
   FRESHLY GROUND PEPPER
   PAPRIKA TO TASTE
2 CUPS LIGHT CREAM

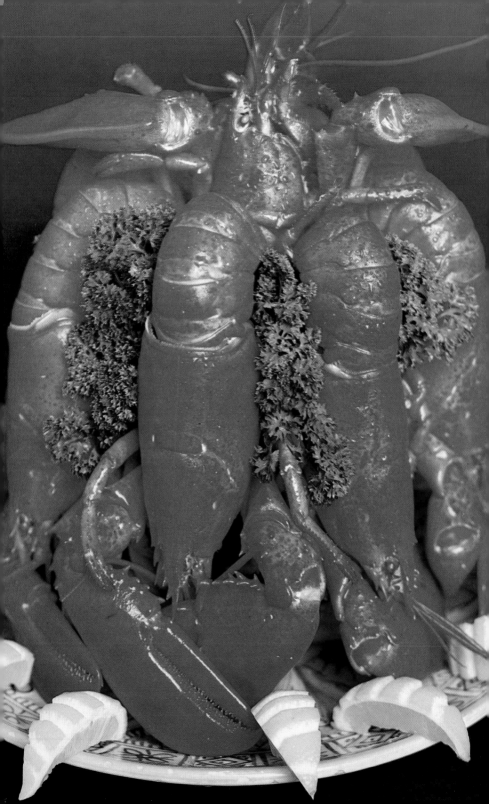

In a heavy, medium size saucepan, melt the butter over high heat, until it begins to foam. Reduce the heat to medium, add the onions and the green pepper; cover and simmer the vegetables for 3 minutes, stirring occasionally.

Add the potatoes, the fish stock, the reserved liquid from the clams, the herbs and season to taste with salt and pepper.

Bring the liquid to a boil over high heat.

Reduce the heat to medium and simmer the chowder, uncovered, until the potatoes are cooked.

Add the clams to the chowder and simmer for 3 to 4 minutes.

Correct the seasonings, mix in the cream and the paprika and serve.

Cold Soups

77
Vichyssoise

For 4 people

---

5 CUPS PARMENTIER CREAM SOUP [*Recipe 71*]
½ TO 1 CUP HEAVY CREAM
1 TABLESPOON FRESH CHIVES, FINELY CHOPPED

Add ½ to 1 cup heavy cream to the Parmentier cream soup, and mix well.

Cover the soup with buttered wax paper and refrigerate overnight.

Serve the soup chilled, and garnished with the fresh chives.

78

Gazpacho

For 4 people

  I CUCUMBER, PEELED AND SEEDED, THINLY SLICED
     SALT
  5 GARLIC CLOVES SMASHED AND FINELY CHOPPED
¼ TEASPOON CUMIN SEEDS
¼ CUP GROUND ALMONDS
  2 TABLESPOONS WINE VINEGAR
¼ CUP OLIVE OIL
  3 TOMATOES PEELED, SEEDED AND CUT IN TWO
2½ CUPS COLD BASIC BROWN BEEF STOCK [*Recipes 15 or 16*]
     FRESHLY GROUND PEPPER
½ GREEN PEPPER, SEEDED AND THINLY SLICED
  I TABLESPOON FRESH PARSLEY, FINELY CHOPPED

Place the cucumber slices in a mixing bowl. Sprinkle the cucumber with salt and set aside for 30 minutes.

Drain the cucumber slices.

Blend the garlic, cumin seeds and the ground almonds together.

Pour in the vinegar and the olive oil; blend once again.

Add the cucumbers and the tomatoes, blend well.

Pour in the beef stock and blend thoroughly.

Season the gazpacho to taste.

Cover the gazpacho with buttered wax paper and refrigerate for at least 4 to 5 hours.

Pour the gazpacho into a soup tureen and garnish with the green pepper and parsley.

Beautiful Eggs

79
Eggs à la Française

For 1 person

2 LARGE EGGS
1 TEASPOON BUTTER
SALT
FRESHLY GROUND WHITE PEPPER

Carefully break the eggs into a dish.

In a small crêpe pan, melt the butter over very low heat.
When the butter is melted, but barely lukewarm, gently slide the eggs into the pan.

Cook the eggs over very low heat, uncovered, until the egg white is the color of milk and completely firm.

Season well with salt and freshly ground pepper.

Transfer to a heated plate and serve immediately.

80
Eggs with Cream

For 1 person

2 LARGE EGGS
2 TABLESPOONS HEAVY CREAM OR LIGHT CREAM
1 TEASPOON BUTTER
SALT
FRESHLY GROUND WHITE PEPPER

Preheat the oven to 300°.

Slowly melt the butter in a custard dish, over very low heat.

Carefully break the eggs into the custard dish.

Cover the eggs with the cream.

Bake the eggs in the oven, in a bain marie, for 8 to 10 minutes, or until the egg white is firm.

Season with salt and freshly ground white pepper and serve immediately.

81
Scrambled Eggs

For 2 people

---

4 LARGE EGGS
2 TABLESPOONS BUTTER
2 TABLESPOONS LIGHT CREAM
SALT
FRESHLY GROUND WHITE PEPPER

Half fill the bottom part of a double boiler with water and bring the water to a boil.

In a mixing bowl, lightly beat the eggs and cream

In a mixing bowl, lightly beat the eggs and cream together with a fork.

Melt the butter in the top part of the double boiler.

Pour the eggs into the melted butter, place over the bottom half of the double boiler and cook the eggs slowly, whisking constantly, until they become creamy.

Transfer the eggs to a heated platter and season with salt and pepper.

Serve immediately.

82
Eggs Chasseur

Recommended as an intimate brunch for two

---

  5 SLICES BACON, CUT INTO SMALL PIECES
12 MUSHROOMS, QUARTERED
   SALT
   FRESHLY GROUND PEPPER
½ TEASPOON FRESH PARSLEY, FINELY CHOPPED
  4 LARGE EGGS
  2 TABLESPOONS BUTTER
  2 TABLESPOONS LIGHT CREAM

In a sauté pan, cook the bacon over high heat for 2 to 3 minutes, stirring frequently.

Add the mushrooms to the bacon, season to taste and sauté the mushrooms, uncovered, for 4 minutes, stirring frequently.

Remove the sauté pan from the heat.

Prepare the scrambled eggs *(Recipe 81)*.
Transfer the scrambled eggs to a heated platter.

Spoon the bacon-mushroom mixture onto the scrambled eggs, and garnish with the chopped parsley.

Serve immediately.

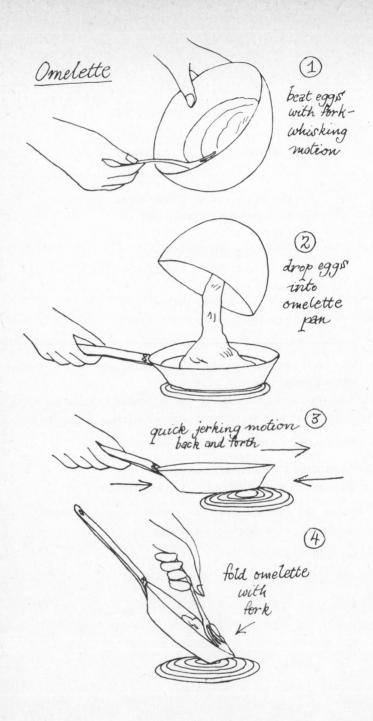

Omelette

① beat eggs
with fork -
whisking
motion

② drop eggs
into
omelette
pan

quick jerking motion ③
back and forth →

④ fold omelette
with
fork

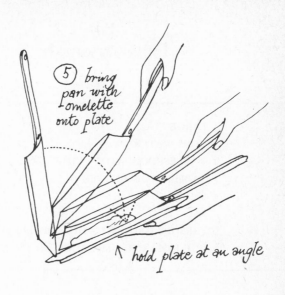

⑤ bring pan with omelette onto plate

↑ hold plate at an angle

With Filling

mushrooms on a plate ① (could be any kind of filling)

place mushrooms (or filling) in the middle of omelette ②

fold over ③

83
Eggs Orientale

For 4 people

---

4 LARGE EGGS
3 CUPS WATER
1 TABLESPOON WHITE VINEGAR
1 TABLESPOON BUTTER
4 SLICES TOMATO, 1½" THICK
  SALT
  FRESHLY GROUND WHITE PEPPER
½ CUP HOLLANDAISE SAUCE [*Recipe 35*]

Preheat the oven to Broil.

In a saucepan, bring the water and the vinegar to a boil.

Break the eggs into a dish and gently slide the eggs into the boiling liquid.

Poach the eggs for 3½ minutes.

Remove the eggs from the liquid with a slotted spoon and set them aside in a warm platter.

In a saucepan, melt the butter over high heat, until it begins to foam. Reduce the heat to medium high and sauté the tomato slices in the butter, for 2 minutes on each side.

Arrange the tomato slices in a buttered baking dish.
Place the egg on each tomato slice and season well.
Cover the eggs with Hollandaise sauce.

Bake the eggs in the oven, 4" away from the broiling element, for 2 to 3 minutes.

Serve immediately.

84

The Art of Making Omelettes

For 1 person

Use an omelette pan, which is an 8" steel frying pan with rounded edges.

You should only use the omelette pan for making omelettes. The pan should never be scrubbed, but should simply be wiped clean after use.

---

2 OR 3 LARGE EGGS
1 TABLESPOON LIGHT CREAM, OR WATER
1 TABLESPOON BUTTER
SALT
FRESHLY GROUND WHITE PEPPER

In a mixing bowl, lightly beat the eggs, cream (or water), salt and pepper together, with a fork.

Melt the butter in the omelette pan, over very high heat. The butter should coat the bottom of the pan.

As soon as the butter stops foaming, add the beaten eggs. Cook the omelette over very high heat.

Shake the pan often until the eggs are almost set.

With a fork or spoon, gently bring the right side of the omelette towards the middle.

If you wish to stuff the omelette, you should spoon the warm stuffing into the middle of the omelette at this point.

Carefully slide the omelette towards the left hand side until the edge of the omelette overhangs by ½".

Turn the omelette upside down on a warmed dish and serve immediately.

85
Cheese Omelette

For 1 person

OMELETTE [*Recipe 84*]
STUFFING: 2 TABLESPOONS GRATED CHEESE

86
Mushroom Omelette

For 1 person

OMELETTE [*Recipe 84*]
STUFFING:
    1 TEASPOON BUTTER
    6 MUSHROOMS THINLY SLICED
       SALT
       FRESHLY GROUND PEPPER

In a small sauté pan, melt the butter over high heat, until it begins to foam.

Reduce the heat to medium-high and sauté the sliced mushrooms, uncovered, for 3 minutes, stirring frequently.

Season the mushrooms with salt and pepper.

Reserve 3 mushroom slices.

Spoon the mushrooms onto the omelette.

Once the omelette has been transferred to a warmed dish, make 3 incisions in the omelette and decorate by inserting the reserved mushroom slices into the incisions.

Economical Dishes

87
Beef Sautéed with Onions

For 2 people

---

    1 POUND LEFTOVER ROAST BEEF OR
        1 POUND UNCOOKED TOP ROUND IN 2" SLICES
        CUT AT AN ANGLE
1½ ONIONS, THINLY SLICED
  2 TABLESPOONS BUTTER
    SALT
  1 TEASPOON WINE VINEGAR
  1 TABLESPOON FRESH PARSLEY, FINELY CHOPPED

In a sauté pan, melt the butter over high heat until it begins to foam. Add the cooked beef and sauté for 2 minutes on each side; OR, add the raw beef and sauté for 3 minutes on each side.

Season the beef with salt and pepper, to taste.

Set the beef aside on a heated platter.

Add the onions to the sauté pan and cook them over very high heat until golden brown, stirring frequently.
Return the beef to the pan and rewarm it for a few seconds.

Correct the seasonings and mix in the wine vinegar.

Garnish with the chopped parsley.

88
Mushrooms à la Crème on Toast

For 2 people

½ POUND MUSHROOMS
¼ TABLESPOON BUTTER
  SALT
  FRESHLY GROUND PEPPER
2 DRIED SHALLOTS, FINELY CHOPPED
4 TABLESPOONS DRY VERMOUTH [OPTIONAL]
1 CUP HOT WHITE SAUCE THICK [*Recipe 25*]
2 SLICES TOASTED FRENCH BREAD
1 TABLESPOON GRATED MOZZARELLA CHEESE
1 TABLESPOON FRESH PARSLEY, FINELY CHOPPED

Preheat the oven to Broil.

In a sauté pan, melt the butter over high heat until it begins to foam. Reduce the heat to medium, add the mushrooms, and cook for 5 minutes, uncovered, stirring occasionally.

Season the mushrooms with salt and pepper.

Add the shallots to the mushrooms and pour in the vermouth. Increase the heat to high and reduce the liquid, uncovered, for 2 minutes.

Mix the white sauce into the mushrooms and correct the seasonings.

Arrange the toasted French bread in a baking dish.
Spoon the mushrooms à la crème onto the toasted bread.

Sprinkle with grated cheese.

Broil the mushrooms, 4" away from the broiling element, for 3 to 4 minutes.

Garnish with the chopped parsley and serve immediately.

89
Macaroni à la Barbara

For 2 people

½ POUND MACARONI
2 TABLESPOONS BUTTER
1 POUND MUSHROOMS, WASHED AND SLICED
SALT
FRESHLY GROUND PEPPER
1½ CUPS HOT QUICK TOMATO SAUCE [*Recipe 33*]
½ CUP GRATED MOZZARELLA CHEESE

Preheat the oven to Broil.

Drop the macaroni into a stockpot half-filled with boiling, salted water. Cook the macaroni, uncovered, for 10 minutes. Rinse the macaroni under running water for 6 minutes, drain and set aside.

In a sauté pan, melt 2 tablespoons butter over high heat, until it begins to foam.
Reduce the heat to medium, add the mushrooms and cook, uncovered, for 5 minutes, stirring occasionally. Season the mushrooms with salt and pepper.

Rewarm the macaroni by placing it in a large sieve and immersing the sieve in hot water, for 4 minutes.
Drain the macaroni.

In a buttered baking dish, alternate layers of macaroni, mushrooms and tomato sauce. Finish with a layer of macaroni and cover with the grated cheese.

Bake the macaroni, uncovered, for 15 minutes, in the middle of the oven.

90
Roast Beef à l'Italienne

For 4 people

½ TO 1 POUND LEFTOVER ROAST BEEF, THINLY SLICED
2 BOSTON LETTUCES, WASHED AND WELL DRAINED
   RESERVE THE LETTUCE HEARTS
¾ POUND WHOLE GREEN BEANS
2 COOKED POTATOES, PEELED AND SLICED
12 CHERRY TOMATOES, CUT IN TWO
   FRESH PARSLEY OR WATERCRESS
   SALT
   FRESHLY GROUND PEPPER
½ CUP VINAIGRETTE [*Recipe 37*]

Drop the green beans into a large saucepan filled with boiling, salted water. Cover and blanch the green beans for 10 minutes. Remove the saucepan from the heat and cool the green beans under running water for at least 4 minutes.
Drain on paper towels.

Dry off the lettuce leaves with paper towels or in a salad dryer.

Arrange the lettuce leaves in the middle of the salad bowl.
Arrange the green beans, in a ring, around the lettuce.
Surround the beans by the roast beef slices.

Surround the roast beef with the potato slices, by leaning the potato slices against the inner wall of the salad bowl.

Arrange the cherry tomatoes alongside the potato slices.

Garnish the salad with the fresh parsley or watercress and the reserved lettuce hearts.

Before serving, season the salad with salt and pepper and mix in the vinaigrette.

91
One for Three

For 4 people

---

3 TABLESPOONS BUTTER
1 POUND BEEF TENDERLOIN THINLY SLICED AT AN
   ANGLE
1 SMALL ONION, PEELED AND THINLY SLICED
1 GREEN PEPPER, SEEDED AND THINLY SLICED
1 GARLIC CLOVE, SMASHED AND FINELY CHOPPED
1 POUND MUSHROOMS, THINLY SLICED
2 WATER CHESTNUTS, THINLY SLICED
8 TOMATO WEDGES
  SALT
  FRESHLY GROUND PEPPER

In a sauté pan, melt the butter over high heat until it begins to foam. Add the beef and sauté, uncovered, over high heat, for 3 minutes, stirring frequently.
Set the beef aside on a heated platter.

Immediately add the onions, green pepper and garlic clove to the pan; sauté for 2 minutes, uncovered. Add the mushrooms, and sauté for 2 minutes, stirring frequently.

Add the water chestnuts and the tomato wedges, and sauté for one minute. Season to taste with salt and pepper.

Return the meat, along with the juices which have formed in the platter, to the vegetables and rewarm the beef for a few seconds.

Correct the seasonings.

Arrange on top of a bed of rice, and serve immediately.

92
Halibut Casserole
For 4 people

---

  2 POUNDS HALIBUT
     JUICE OF 1 LEMON
  1 PINCH THYME
  1 BAY LEAF
  2 TABLESPOONS WHITE VINEGAR
     SALT
     FRESHLY GROUND PEPPER
  2 CUPS HOT WHITE SAUCE THICK [*Recipe 25*]
 ½ CUP MEDIUM STRONG CHEDDAR CHEESE, GRATED

Preheat the oven to Broil.

In a large buttered pan, or baking dish, place the halibut, lemon juice, thyme, bay leaf and vinegar.
Add cold water to cover and season with salt and pepper.
Cover with foil or buttered wax paper. Gently press the paper down with your fingertips so that the paper touches the surface of the ingredients.

Bring the liquid to a boil over high heat. Reduce the heat to low and simmer the halibut for:

    20 minutes, if the halibut is cut into 1" slices, or
    15 minutes per pound, if the halibut is in one piece.

Remove the halibut from the baking dish and reserve the cooking liquor.
Flake the halibut into a mixing bowl.
Mix in the white sauce, and 2 tablespoons of the reserved cooking liquor.

Pour the mixture into a buttered baking dish. Sprinkle with the grated cheese.
Bake the halibut casserole, uncovered, for 15 to 20 minutes, in the middle of the oven.

93
Hamburger à la Ritz

For 4 people

---

1   POUND LEAN GROUND MEAT SHAPED INTO 4
    PATTIES
2   TABLESPOONS BUTTER
4   SLICES TOMATO, ½" THICK
    SALT
    FRESHLY GROUND PEPPER
4   TOASTED HAMBURGER BUNS
½   CUP BEARNAISE SAUCE [*Recipe 34*]

In a sauté pan, melt the butter over high heat.
When the foam subsides, add the beef patties and sauté the patties
on one side, for 2 minutes.

Turn the patties over, and add the tomato slices. Sauté the tomato
slices for one minute on each side.

Season the tomato slices and the patties.

Place a slice of tomato and a patty on each hamburger bun, and
cover with béarnaise sauce.

94
Quiche Maison

Yield: 4 to 6 slices

9" PIE SHELL [*Recipe 171*]
5 SLICES BACON [OPTIONAL]
½ CUP GRATED GRUYÈRE CHEESE
4 LARGE EGGS OR
   5 MEDIUM SIZE EGGS
1 TABLESPOON FRESH PARSLEY FINELY CHOPPED
1½ CUPS HEAVY CREAM
   SALT
   FRESHLY GROUND PEPPER
   A PINCH OF NUTMEG

Bake the pastry shell at 400° for 10 minutes.
Remove the pastry shell from the oven and let cool.

Preheat the oven to 375°.

Blanch the bacon in a saucepan filled with boiling water, for 3 to 4 minutes.

Dice the bacon and drain on paper towels.

Place the diced bacon in a sauté pan and cook it, uncovered, over high heat, for 3 minutes.
Drain the bacon on paper towels.
Place the bacon in the pie shell and cover it with the grated cheese.

In a mixing bowl, beat the eggs, parsley, cream, salt, pepper and nutmeg together with a whisk.

Pour this mixture into the pie shell.

If this mixture is not sufficient to fill the pie shell, complete with milk or cream.

Bake the quiche maison for 30 to 35 minutes, or until a knife inserted in the middle of the quiche comes out clean.

95
Les Saucisses à l'Italienne

For 4 people

---

12 UNCOOKED PORK SAUSAGES
10 OUNCES SPAGHETTI
 2 TABLESPOONS BUTTER
½ POUND MUSHROOMS, SLICED
 1 ONION, THINLY SLICED
 1 GARLIC CLOVE, SMASHED AND FINELY CHOPPED
    SALT
    FRESHLY GROUND PEPPER
 2 CUPS HOT QUICK TOMATO SAUCE [*Recipe 33*]

Preheat the oven to Broil.

Drop the pork sausages into a large saucepan three-quarters filled with boiling water; cook, uncovered, for 5 minutes, over very high heat.
Drain and set aside.

Drop the spaghetti into a stockpot half-filled with boiling, salted water and cook the spaghetti, uncovered, over very high heat, for 10 minutes,
Rinse the spaghetti under running water for at least 6 minutes.
Drain the spaghetti and set it aside.

In a heavy, medium size saucepan, melt the butter over high heat, until it begins to foam. Reduce the heat to medium high, add the onions and sauté, uncovered, for 2 minutes, stirring frequently. Add the mushrooms and the garlic to the onions, season to taste with salt and pepper and cook, uncovered, over high heat, for 5 to 6 minutes, stirring frequently. Add the tomato sauce.

Bring the sauce to a boil over high heat. Reduce the heat to medium and simmer the sauce, uncovered, for 15 minutes.

Brown the pork sausages, 6" away from the broiling element, for 3 to 4 minutes on each side.

Rewarm the spaghetti by placing it in a large sieve and immersing the sieve in hot water, for 4 minutes.
Drain the spaghetti.

Spoon the spaghetti into four heated plates.

Arrange 3 pork sausages in each plate, on top of the spaghetti.
Spoon the sauce over the sausages and the spaghetti.

Souffles & Fondues

96
Cheese Soufflé

For 4 people

3 TABLESPOONS BUTTER
3 TABLESPOONS FLOUR
I CUP BOILING MILK
4 EGG YOLKS
  SALT
  FRESHLY GROUND WHITE PEPPER
  A DASH CAYENNE PEPPER
5 EGG WHITES
I CUP GRUYÈRE OR STRONG CHEDDAR CHEESE, GRATED
  SIX-CUP SOUFFLE DISH

Preheat the oven to 375°.

Butter the soufflé dish and sprinkle it with a bit of grated cheese.

In a small, heavy, saucepan, melt the butter over low heat.
Add the flour to the butter and cook the "roux", uncovered, for 3 minutes, stirring constantly.

Remove the saucepan from the heat, add the boiling milk to the "roux" and mix well with a wooden spoon.

Return the saucepan to the heat and cook the sauce, uncovered, for 2 to 3 minutes, over low heat, stirring constantly with a wooden spoon.

Remove the saucepan from the heat and add the egg yolks, one at a time, mixing until each egg yolk is thoroughly blended before adding the next one.
Season the mixture with salt, pepper and cayenne pepper.

In a mixing bowl, beat the egg whites until very stiff. Blend 3 tablespoons egg white into the sauce, with a rubber spatula. Mix the grated cheese into the sauce.

Using a rubber spatula, gently fold the remaining beaten egg whites into the cheese sauce.

Carefully pour the mixture into the prepared soufflé dish.

Bake the soufflé for 30 minutes, in the middle of the oven.

97
Potato Soufflé

For 4 people

---

    10 OUNCES RAW POTATOES, SCRUBBED
     2 TABLESPOONS BUTTER
    ¾ CUP LIGHT CREAM
     4 EGG YOLKS AND 5 EGG WHITES
        SALT
        FRESHLY GROUND PEPPER
        A DASH CAYENNE PEPPER
        A DASH NUTMEG

        SIX-CUP SOUFFLÉ DISH, BUTTERED

Preheat the oven to 375°.

Drop the potatoes into a saucepan filled with boiling, salted water and cook until they are tender.
Cool the potatoes under running water for at least 4 minutes.
Peel the potatoes and rub them through a sieve, into a heavy saucepan.

Cook the potatoes, uncovered, over medium heat, for 2 to 3 minutes, stirring constantly, in order to remove the excess water.
Mix the cream and the butter into the potatoes.

Remove the saucepan from the heat and add the egg yolks to the potatoes, one at a time, mixing until each egg yolk is thoroughly blended before adding the next one.
Season the mixture with salt, pepper, cayenne pepper and nutmeg.

Beat the egg whites until very stiff.

Blend 3 tablespoons of beaten egg white into the potato mixture with a rubber spatula. Gently fold the remaining egg whites into the mixture with a rubber spatula.

Carefully pour the mixture into the buttered soufflé dish.
Bake the soufflé for 25 minutes, in the middle of the oven.

98
Party Beef Fondue

---

6 OUNCES FILET [THE SMALLER END OF THE BEEF
  TENDERLOIN]
  CUT INTO 1" CUBES, PER PERSON
¼ CUP HOT BÉARNAISE SAUCE, PER PERSON
  [*Recipe 34*]
¼ CUP HOT BOURGUIGNON SAUCE, PER PERSON
  [RECIPE 30]
¼ CUP AILLOLI, PER PERSON [*Recipe 49*]

WE RECOMMEND THAT YOU USE PEANUT OIL.

Serve the beef fondue with mushroom caps broiled with garlic
butter (Recipe 8).

99
Cheese Fondu

For 4 people

---

1 POUND GRUYÈRE CHEESE, DICED
½ POUND EMMENTHAL CHEESE, DICED
1 GARLIC CLOVE, PEELED
3 OUNCES KIRSCH
¼ CUP [SCANT] WHITE WINE
1 TEASPOON CORNSTARCH
  SALT
  FRESHLY GROUND WHITE PEPPER
  A PINCH NUTMEG
  FRENCH BREAD CUT INTO 1" CUBES

Rub the inside of an earthenware fondue dish with the garlic clove and then discard the garlic clove.

Mix the kirsch, the white wine and the cornstarch together.

Light the burner under the fondue dish.

Melt the cheese in the fondue dish, over the burner, stirring constantly.

When the cheese begins to melt, stir in the kirsch-cornstarch-wine mixture. Season the fondue to taste with salt, pepper and nutmeg.

Stir constantly until the fondue becomes thick.

Serve with the French bread cubes.

Fish

100
Lake Trout Baked in Foil

For 4 people

3 POUND LAKE TROUT, CLEANED
3 TABLESPOONS BUTTER
1 ONION THINLY SLICED
2 DRIED SHALLOTS FINELY CHOPPED
1 CARROT, THINLY SLICED
  SALT
  FRESHLY GROUND PEPPER
¼ TEASPOON THYME
1 BAY LEAF
  FEW FENNEL SEEDS
¼ CUP DRY WHITE WINE

4 TABLESPOONS WATER
JUICE OF ½ LEMON
1 PARSLEY SPRIG
LEMON WEDGES

Preheat the oven to 350°.

In a saucepan, melt the butter over high heat, until it begins to foam. Reduce the heat to medium, add the onions, shallots, carrots and herbs and simmer, uncovered, for 4 minutes, stirring frequently.

Season the vegetables with salt and pepper. Pour in the white wine, the water and the lemon juice and add the parsley sprig.

Bring the liquid to a boil over high heat. Reduce the heat to medium and simmer the liquid for 5 minutes. Remove the saucepan from the heat and set aside.

Wash the lake trout under cold running water.
Drain the trout on paper towels.

Place the lake trout in the middle of a large piece of foil. Fold the paper loosely over the trout and securely fold one edge of the foil.
Pour the ingredients from the saucepan into the open end of the foil.
Seal the liquid in the foil by securely folding the remaining edge of the paper.

Place the trout in a baking dish.

Bake the trout for 45 minutes (or 15 minutes per pound).

Remove the trout from the oven.

Open one end of foil and pour out the cooking liquor.
Reserve the liquor.

Unwrap the trout and carefully transfer it onto a heated serving platter.

Pour the cooking liquor and the vegetables over the trout.

Decorate with lemon wedges.

101
Pickerel à la Coker

For 4 people

---

4 ½ POUND PICKEREL FILETS
1 CUP MILK
   SALT
1 CUP FLOUR
3 TABLESPOONS BUTTER
1 TABLESPOON OLIVE OIL
   JUICE OF ½ LEMON
2 TABLESPOONS CAPERS
   FRESHLY GROUND PEPPER
1 TABLESPOON FRESH PARSLEY, FINELY CHOPPED

Preheat the oven to 350°.

Wash the pickerel filets under cold running water and drain on paper towels.

In a mixing bowl, combine 1 cup milk and ¼ teaspoon salt.

Dip the filets in the salted milk and then in the flour.
Gently shake off the excess flour.
Put the filets aside on a sheet of wax paper.

Place 2 tablespoons butter and 1 tablespoon olive oil in a sauté pan with an ovenproof, or metal handle, over high heat. As soon as the foam subsides, add the filets and reduce the heat to medium.

Cook the filets, uncovered, for 4 to 5 minutes on each side.
Season the filets with salt and pepper.
Place the sauté pan in the oven, uncovered and bake the filets for 5 to 6 minutes, or until the flesh is firm to the touch.

Transfer the filets to a heated platter.

Pour off the fat from the sauté pan.

Melt the remaining tablespoon of butter in the sauté pan and brown the butter over medium heat, uncovered, for 1 minute.

Add the lemon juice, capers and parsley to the butter.

Pour the sauce over the filets and serve immediately.

102
Filet of Perch with Mushrooms

For 4 people

---

8 ¼ POUND PERCH FILETS
1 EGG
1 CUP MILK
SALT
1 CUP FLOUR
3 TABLESPOONS CLARIFIED BUTTER OR
   3 TABLESPOONS VEGETABLE OIL
FRESHLY GROUND PEPPER
1 TABLESPOON BUTTER
½ POUND MUSHROOMS, SLICED
JUICE OF ½ LEMON
1 TABLESPOON FRESH PARSLEY, FINELY CHOPPED

Wash the perch filets under cold running water and drain them on paper towels.

Lightly beat the egg in a large mixing bowl. Add the milk and ¼ teaspoon of salt to the egg and mix well.

Dip the filets in the egg-milk mixture and then in the flour. Gently shake off the excess flour.

Put the filets aside on a sheet of wax paper.

Place the clarified butter or oil in a sauté pan, over high heat. When the butter or oil is hot, add the perch filets and sauté the filets over high heat, uncovered, for 4 minutes on each side. Season the filets with salt and pepper.

Transfer the filets to a heated serving platter.

Pour off the fat from the sauté pan.
Melt 1 tablespoon fresh butter in the sauté pan, over high heat until the butter begins to foam. Reduce the heat to medium, add the mushrooms, and cook, uncovered, for 5 minutes, stirring occasionally.
Add the lemon juice and the parsley to the mushrooms and season to taste with salt and pepper.

Spoon the mushrooms over the perch filets and serve immediately.

103
Lake Trout Amandine

For 4 people

---

4 10 OUNCE LAKE TROUT, CLEANED
1 EGG
1 CUP MILK
   SALT
1 CUP FLOUR
3 TABLESPOONS CLARIFIED BUTTER OR
      3 TABLESPOONS VEGETABLE OIL
   FRESHLY GROUND PEPPER
1 TABLESPOON BUTTER
2 TABLESPOONS FLAKED ALMONDS
   JUICE OF ½ LEMON
1 TABLESPOON FRESH PARSLEY, FINELY CHOPPED

Preheat the oven to 350°.

Wash the trout under cold running water and drain them on paper towels. Season the inside of the trout with salt and pepper.

Lightly beat the egg in a large mixing bowl. Add the milk and ¼ teaspoon of salt to the egg and mix well.

Dip the trout in the egg-milk mixture and then in the flour. Gently shake off the excess flour.
Put the trout aside on a sheet of wax paper.

Place the clarified butter or oil in a sauté pan with an ovenproof or metal handle, over high heat. When the butter or oil is hot, add the trout and sauté them over high heat, uncovered, for 4 to 5 minutes on each side. Season the trout with salt and pepper.

Place the sauté pan in the oven and bake the trout, uncovered, for 5 to 6 minutes.

Transfer the trout to a heated platter.

Pour off the fat from the sauté pan.
Melt 1 tablespoon fresh butter in the sauté pan, over medium heat and brown the butter for 1 minute.

Add the flaked almonds to the butter and cook the almonds for 1 minute.

Add the lemon juice and the chopped parsley to the almonds.

Pour the sauce over the lake trout.

104
Salmon Poached in Court Bouillon

For 4 people

---

4 SLICES OF SALMON, 1″ THICK
COURT BOUILLON [*Recipe 19*]
3 TABLESPOONS BUTTER
JUICE OF ½ LEMON
1 TABLESPOON FRESH PARSLEY, FINELY CHOPPED
SALT
FRESHLY GROUND PEPPER

Place the salmon slices in the bottom of a baking dish.
If you have a fish poacher (poissonière), place the fish on the grid and lower it to the bottom of the fish poacher.

Cover the salmon with court bouillon.

Cover and bring the court bouillon to a slow simmer over medium heat.

Simmer the salmon in the court bouillon for 15 to 20 minutes.

Transfer the salmon to a heated serving platter and season.

Pour 2 tablespoons of court bouillon into a small saucepan. Reduce the court bouillon over high heat, for one minute. Whisk in 3 tablespoons of fresh butter.
Remove the saucepan from the heat.

Add the lemon juice and the chopped parsley to the sauce and pour over the salmon.

105
Poached Salmon
with Mousseline Sauce

For 4 people

---

4 SLICES SALMON 1" THICK
COURT BOUILLON [*Recipe 19*]
SALT
FRESHLY GROUND PEPPER
1 CUP MOUSSELINE SAUCE [*Recipe 36*]

Arrange the salmon slices in the bottom of a baking dish. If you have a fish poacher (poissonnière), place the fish on the grid and lower it to the bottom of the fish poacher.

Cover the salmon with court bouillon.

Cover and bring the court bouillon to a slow simmer over medium heat.

Simmer the salmon in the court bouillon for 15 to 20 minutes.

Transfer the salmon to a heated serving platter and season.

Serve with the mousseline sauce.

106
Poached Halibut with Mushroom Sauce

For 4 people

---

4 SLICES HALIBUT 1" THICK
COURT BOUILLON [*Recipe 19*]
SALT
FRESHLY GROUND PEPPER

THE SAUCE
  1/2 POUND MUSHROOMS, SLICED
  2 TABLESPOONS BUTTER
  I DRIED SHALLOT FINELY CHOPPED
  I CUP HOT BASIC WHITE SAUCE THIN [*Recipe 24*]
  2 TABLESPOONS HOT COURT BOUILLON
    SALT
    FRESHLY GROUND PEPPER

Arrange the halibut slices in the bottom of a baking dish. If you have a fish poacher (poissonnière), place the fish on the grid and lower it to the bottom of the fish poacher.

Cover the halibut with court bouillon.

Cover and bring the court bouillon to a slow simmer over medium heat.

Simmer the halibut in the court bouillon for 15 to 20 minutes.

While the halibut is cooking, melt 2 tablespoons of butter in a medium size, heavy saucepan, over high heat. When the butter begins to foam, add the chopped shallots, reduce the heat to medium and cook the shallots, uncovered, for one minute.

Add the sliced mushrooms to the shallots and cook, uncovered, for 3 to 4 minutes, stirring occasionally.

Mix in the white sauce and 2 tablespoons of court bouillon.

Season the mushroom sauce to taste.

Transfer the halibut to a heated serving platter.

Season the halibut.

Pour the mushroom sauce over the halibut.

107
Cod au Gratin

For 4 people

---

2 POUNDS COD FILET
  COURT BOUILLON [*Recipe 19*]
2 CUPS HOT WHITE SAUCE THICK [*Recipe 25*]
  SALT
  FRESHLY GROUND WHITE PEPPER
  A DASH OF CAYENNE PEPPER
½ CUP GRATED CHEESE

Preheat the oven to Broil.

Wash the cod under cold running water.

Place the cod in a buttered pan, season with salt and pepper and cover with the court bouillon.

Cover the pan with buttered fireproof paper. Press the paper down with your fingertips so that it covers the cod.

Bring the court bouillon to a boil over medium heat, on top of the stove. Then reduce heat and simmer the cod for 30 minutes (or 15 minutes per pound).

When the fish is almost done, pour 2 to 3 tablespoons of hot court bouillon into a medium size saucepan. Reduce the court bouillon for one minute, over very high heat.

Add the white sauce to the 2 tablespoons of court bouillon, mix well and season the sauce with salt, pepper and cayenne pepper.

Remove the saucepan from the heat.

Transfer the cod to a buttered baking dish. Pour the sauce over the cod and cover with the grated cheese.

Broil the cod, 6" away from the broiling element, for 6 to 7 minutes.

108
Cod à l'Espagnole

For 4 people

---

    2 POUNDS COD
    2 TABLESPOONS BUTTER
    1 GREEN PEPPER, SEEDED AND THINLY SLICED
    1/2 POUND MUSHROOMS, SLICED
      PINCH THYME
    1/2 TEASPOON TARRAGON
    1/2 TEASPOON CHERVIL
      PINCH OF FENNEL SEEDS
    8 TOMATO WEDGES
      A BAY LEAF
      SALT
      FRESHLY GROUND PEPPER
    1/2 CUP DRY WHITE WINE
    1 CUP WATER
      JUICE OF 1/2 LEMON
    1 TABLESPOON FRESH PARSLEY, FINELY CHOPPED

Preheat the oven to 350°.

In a sauté pan, melt the butter over high heat, until it begins to foam. Add the green pepper, the mushrooms, the thyme, tarragon, chervil and fennel seeds; reduce the heat to medium and cook, uncovered, for 4 minutes, stirring occasionally. Add the tomato wedges and the bay leaf and cook, uncovered, for one minute. Season to taste and remove the pan from the heat.

Wash the cod under cold running water and pat dry with paper towels.
Season the cod with salt and pepper and place it in a buttered baking dish.
Pour the contents of the sauté pan over the cod.

Add the white wine and the water and correct the seasonings.
Cover the baking dish with aluminium foil.

Bake the cod for 30 minutes.

Transfer the cod to a heated serving platter.
Place the baking dish over high heat and reduce the sauce, on top of the stove, for 3 to 4 minutes.
Squeeze the lemon juice into the sauce. Discard the bay leaf.

Pour the sauce over the cod.
Garnish with the chopped parsley.

109
Broiled Filet of Porgy
with Shallot Butter

For 4 people

---

4 8 OUNCE PORGY FILETS
2 TABLESPOONS VEGETABLE OIL
   SALT
   FRESHLY GROUND PEPPER
   JUICE OF ½ LEMON
4 TEASPOONS SHALLOT BUTTER [*Recipe 9*]

Preheat the oven to Broil.

Wash the porgy filets under cold running water.
Dry the filets with paper towels.

Brush the filets with the vegetable oil.
Season the filets with salt and pepper.

Arrange the filets in a baking dish.

Broil the filets, 6" away from the broiling element, for 7 minutes on each side. Baste occasionally with the vegetable oil.

Remove the baking dish from the oven.
Season again with salt and pepper.
Squeeze the lemon juice over the filets.
Place 1 teaspoon of shallot butter on each filet.

Return the filets to the oven and broil until the shallot butter
has melted.

110
Sole Bretonne
For 4 people

---

8 4 OUNCE SOLE FILETS
1½ CUPS MILK
2 EGGS
SALT
FRESHLY GROUND PEPPER
1½ CUPS FLOUR
6 TABLESPOONS BUTTER
½ POUND MUSHROOMS, CUT IN FOUR
¾ POUND COOKED SHRIMP, PEELED, DEVEINED AND
COARSELY DICED [*Recipe 111*]
1 TABLESPOON CAPERS
1 TABLESPOON FRESH PARSLEY, FINELY CHOPPED
JUICE OF ½ LEMON

Wash the sole under cold running water and drain on paper
towels.

In a mixing bowl, blend the milk and eggs together with a whisk.
Season the filets and dip them in the milk-egg mixture and then in
the flour.
Gently shake off the excess flour.

Melt 4 tablespoons butter in a sauté pan, over high heat.
As soon as the foam subsides, add the filets and reduce the heat
to medium.

Cook the filets, uncovered, for 5 minutes on each side.

Season the filets again and transfer them to a heated platter.

Pour off the fat from the sauté pan.

Melt the 2 remaining tablespoons of fresh butter in the sauté pan.
Add the mushrooms and cook, uncovered, over medium heat, for 2 minutes, stirring occasionally.
Add the shrimp to the mushrooms and cook for 2 minutes, uncovered, stirring occasionally.
Season with salt and pepper, add the capers, parsley and lemon juice and pour over the sole.

Crustaceans

111
Technique: How to Cook Shrimp
There are two ways to cook shrimp:

a)--wash the shrimp under cold, running water.

--Drop the shrimp into a large saucepan filled with cold, salted water* and 1 tablespoon of white vinegar (optional).

--Bring the water to a boil over very high heat.

--As soon as the water reaches the boiling point, the shrimp are cooked.

--Immediately cool the shrimp under running water, for at least 4 minutes.

b)--Wash the shrimp under cold, running water.

--Drop the shrimp into a large saucepan filled with boiling, salted water* and 1 tablespoon white vinegar (optional).

--Simmer the shrimp for 3 minutes.

--Immediately cool the shrimp under running water, for at least 4 minutes.

*or court Bouillon (Recipe 19)

If you wish to refrigerate the cooked shrimp, do not remove the shell.

Before using the shrimp, shell and devein, that is, slit the shrimp down the back and remove the black or white intestinal vein. Wash the shrimp under cold running water.

112
Lobster Newburg

For 4 people

---

2 1½ POUND LOBSTERS, COOKED*
1 TABLESPOON BUTTER
1 DRIED SHALLOT, FINELY CHOPPED
   PAPRIKA
6 MUSHROOMS, CUT INTO QUARTERS
⅓ CUP MADEIRA WINE OR
      ⅓ CUP COGNAC
½ CUP HOT COURT BOUILLON [*Recipe 19*]
1 CUP, PLUS 1 TABLESPOON HEAVY CREAM
   SALT
   FRESHLY GROUND PEPPER
2 TABLESPOONS KNEADED BUTTER [MANIÉ BUTTER]
      [RECIPE 12]
1 EGG YOLK

Shell the tail, the claws and the body of the lobster.
Reserve the greenish-brown tomalley (or liver) and the coral.

*Plunge the live lobsters, one at a time, into a large stockpot three-quarters filled with boiling, salted water.
    1 pound lobsters - cook for 16 minutes.
    1½ pound lobsters - cook for 19 minutes.
Cool the lobsters under running water.

Cut the lobster flesh into ¾″ pieces, at an angle.

In a heavy, medium size saucepan, melt the butter over high heat, until it begins to foam. Add the lobster and the chopped dried shallot and sprinkle with paprika.
Reduce the heat to medium and cook, uncovered, for 3 minutes, stirring frequently.
Transfer the lobster to a heated platter.

The Sauce

Increase the heat under the sauté pan to high, add the mushrooms, and sauté, uncovered, for 4 minutes, stirring constantly.
Add the madeira wine (or the cognac) to the mushrooms, bring to a boil over high heat and reduce the spirits for 2 minutes.
Add the court bouillon and reduce for 3 to 4 minutes.
Add 1 cup heavy cream, bring to a boil and reduce for another 3 to 4 minutes.
Whisk in the manié butter, over high heat.

Add the lobster and the liquor which has formed in the platter, to the sauce, Correct the seasonings.

In a small bowl, combine the egg yolk, the remaining tablespoon of heavy cream and the reserved tomalley and coral.
Stir into the sauce.

Serve the lobster Newburg on a bed of rice.

113
Lobster à la Lincoln

For 4 people

---

2 1½ POUND LOBSTERS, COOKED*
3 TABLESPOONS BUTTER
2 DRIED SHALLOTS, FINELY CHOPPED
½ POUND MUSHROOMS, SLICED
1 GARLIC CLOVE, SMASHED AND FINELY CHOPPED
½ TEASPOON TARRAGON
1½ CUPS HOT BASIC WHITE SAUCE THIN [*Recipe 24*]
   SALT
   FRESHLY GROUND PEPPER
   WORCESTERSHIRE SAUCE
1 TEASPOON ENGLISH POWDERED MUSTARD
¼ CUP GRATED MOZZARELLA CHEESE
   PARSLEY SPRIGS
   LEMON WEDGES

Preheat the oven to Broil.

Shell the tail and the claws of the lobster.
Split the lobster in half, lengthwise. Remove the meat from the shell and scrape it clean.
Reserve the liquid, the tomalley and the coral.
Broil the shell 6" away from the broiling element, for 6 to 7 minutes, to remove the moisture.
Set the empty lobster shell aside.

In a sauté pan, melt the butter over high heat, until it begins to foam. Add the shallots, the mushrooms, garlic and tarragon,

*Plunge the live lobsters, one at a time, into a large stockpot three-quarters filled with boiling, salted water.
  1 pound lobsters - cook for 16 minutes.
  1½ pound lobsters - cook for 19 minutes.
Cool the lobsters under running water.

reduce the heat to medium; cook, uncovered, for 4 minutes, stirring frequently.

Pour in the white sauce and add the lobster, the liquor from the lobster, the reserved tomalley and coral.

Season to taste with salt, pepper and worcestershire sauce.

Mix in the English mustard.

Arrange the reserved empty shells in a buttered baking dish.

Spoon the mixture into the shells and sprinkle with the grated cheese.

Broil the Lobster à la Lincoln, 6" away from the broiling element, for 6 minutes.

Garnish with parsley sprigs and lemon wedges.

114
Shrimp Provençale

For 4 people

---

2   POUNDS SHRIMP COOKED, SHELLED AND DEVEINED
    [SIZE, 15 TO 20 SHRIMP PER POUND]
    [*See Recipe 111*]
2   TABLESPOONS VEGETABLE OR OLIVE OIL
1   28 OUNCE CAN TOMATOES, DRAINED AND
    COARSELY CHOPPED
2   GARLIC CLOVES, SMASHED AND FINELY CHOPPED
½   TEASPOON TARRAGON
½   TEASPOON OREGANO
    SALT
    FRESHLY GROUND PEPPER
2   TABLESPOONS BUTTER
1   TABLESPOON FRESH PARSLEY, FINELY CHOPPED

Place the oil in a heavy, medium size saucepan, over high heat.

When the oil is hot, add the tomatoes, garlic cloves, tarragon and oregano, Reduce the heat to medium and cook, uncovered, for 9 to 10 minutes, stirring occasionally.
Season to taste with salt and pepper.

In a deep sauté pan, melt the butter over high heat.
When the foam subsides, add the shrimp and sauté, uncovered, for 2 minutes, stirring frequently.

Mix the tomato sauce into the shrimp and correct the seasonings.

Garnish with chopped parsley.

115
Scampi au Gratin

For 4 people

---

32 SCAMPI [SIZE 18 TO 24 SCAMPI PER POUND]
SALT
FRESHLY GROUND PEPPER
JUICE OF ONE LEMON
½ CUP GARLIC BUTTER* AT ROOM TEMPERATURE
[*Recipe 8*]
½ CUP BREADCRUMBS

Preheat the oven to 400°.

Wash the scampi under cold running water.

Cut the scampi, ¾ of the way through, down the back and remove the black or white intestinal vein.
Open the scampi so that the shell will lie flat on a baking dish.

Arrange the scampi in a buttered baking dish.

Season the scampi with salt and pepper.

Squeeze the lemon juice onto the scampi.

Spread ½ teaspoon of garlic butter onto each scampi.

Sprinkle with breadcrumbs.

Broil the scampi, 6" away from the broiling element, for 8 to 10 minutes.

*This recipe could also be made with shallot butter (Recipe 9)

116
Alaska Crab Legs

For 4 people

---

4 POUNDS CRAB LEGS, CUT INTO 5" PIECES
½ POUND GARLIC BUTTER AT ROOM TEMPERATURE
   [*Recipe 8*]

Preheat the oven to 375°.

Break the crab shell every 2 inches.

Fill a pastry bag with the garlic butter.
Force the butter inside the shell, through the fissures.

Arrange the crab legs in a baking dish.

Place in the oven for 15 minutes.

Serve the crab legs with lemon wedges.

117
Frogs' Legs Provençale

For 4 people

2½ POUNDS FROGS' LEGS [SIZE: 9 FROGS' LEGS
    PER POUND]
1½ CUPS MILK
    SALT
    FRESHLY GROUND PEPPER
  1 CUP FLOUR
  4 TABLESPOONS BUTTER
  1 TABLESPOON VEGETABLE OIL
  3 GARLIC CLOVES, SMASHED AND FINELY CHOPPED
  1 TEASPOON FRESH PARSLEY, FINELY CHOPPED
    JUICE OF ½ LEMON

Wash the frogs' legs under cold running water.
Fold the leg along its joint and secure the wider tip of the leg between the opposite bone and ligament.

In a mixing bowl, combine the milk, ¼ teaspoon salt and freshly ground pepper.
Soak the frogs' legs in the seasoned milk for one hour.

Dip the frogs' legs in the flour and gently shake off the excess flour.
Put the frogs' legs aside on a sheet of wax paper.

Place 2 tablespoons butter and 1 tablespoon oil in a sauté pan, over medium heat. When the foam subsides, add the frogs' legs. For a crisp skin, cook the frogs' legs for 7 to 8 minutes on each side; or
For a skin which is not crisp, cook the frogs' legs for 4 minutes on each side, and then place them in the oven, uncovered, for 4 to 5 minutes, at 350°.

When the frogs' legs are done, transfer them to a heated serving platter and season with salt and pepper.

Pour off the fat from the sauté pan.
Melt the remaining 2 tablespoons of fresh butter in the sauté pan, over medium heat. When the butter begins to foam, add the garlic, the chopped parsley and freshly ground pepper.

Simmer the seasonings for 1 to 2 minutes. Squeeze the lemon juice into the sauce.

Pour the sauce over the frogs' legs.

Beef

118
Technique: How to Roast Beef

TIPS ON ROASTS:

Many cuts of beef are suitable for roasting. The tastiest cut of beef is the rib roast; the ribs give the meat an excellent flavor; however, it is also one of the more expensive cuts of beef.

The eye of round, rump roast and sirloin tip also make excellent roasts. These cuts do not contain bone and fat and are thus more economical than the rib roast.

A good cut of beef should be aged, by your butcher, for 2 to 3 weeks. The aging process increases the tenderness and the flavor. After you purchase a roast, you should wrap it in oiled wax paper.

In the summer, a BONELESS *cut of beef, covered and refrigerated, will keep for 3 days.*

In the winter, the same cut of beef will keep for 4 days.

Those cuts of meat which have not been deboned will keep, wrapped and refrigerated, for a maximum of 5 days.

Ingredients - For 4 people

6 POUND RIB ROAST OR

3 POUND EYE OF ROAST OR

4 POUND RUMP ROAST OR

3 POUND SIRLOIN TIP

¼ TEASPOON BASIL

¼ TEASPOON THYME

½ TEASPOON CHERVIL

FRESHLY GROUND PEPPER

1 TABLESPOON VEGETABLE OIL

SALT

2 TABLESPOONS CARROTS, FINELY CHOPPED

2 TABLESPOONS ONIONS, FINELY CHOPPED

1 TABLESPOON CELERY, FINELY CHOPPED

DRIED SHALLOT, FINELY CHOPPED

BAY LEAF

1½ CUPS HOT BASIC BROWN STOCK [*Recipe 15 or 16*]

Preheat the oven to 450°.

Cut a very thin strip of beef from the roast and cut the strip into ½" pieces.
Mix the basil, thyme and chervil together in a small shallow bowl.

Roll the small pieces of beef in the herbs.
Put the remaining herbs aside.

With a paring knife, make small incisions, at least ½" deep, in the roast and insert a sliver of "herbed" beef in each one.

If you plan to cook a rib roast, insert slivers of "herbed" beef between the ribs.
If the cut of beef which you are roasting does not contain any fat, rub the roast with vegetable oil.
Season the roast with pepper. Do not use salt yet, as it will toughen the roast.

Pour 1 tablespoon of vegetable oil into the roasting pan.

Place the roasting pan in the oven for 3 to 4 minutes, or until the oil is hot.

Put the roast in the roasting pan, fat side up, and return the pan to the oven, for 30 minutes.

Reduce the oven heat to 350°. Season the roast with salt.

Total roasting time, including 30 minutes at 450°:

18 minutes per pound: *Rare*
20 minutes per pound: *Medium-Rare*
24 minutes per pound: *Well Done*

Baste the roast and discard the fat, every 15 minutes.

After the prescribed roasting time, remove the roast from the oven and transfer it to a carving board. Let the roast stand for at least 15 minutes, in order to complete the cooking process and to allow the natural juices of the meat to settle.

During this time, remove all but 2 tablespoons of fat from the roasting pan. Try to retain as much of the beef drippings as possible.

Add the chopped carrots, onions, celery, dry shallot, the reserved herbs and the bay leaf to the contents of the roasting pan.

Cook the vegetables, uncovered, over high heat, for 5 to 6 minutes.

Add the beef stock to the vegetables, and season with salt and pepper.

Pour the contents of the roasting pan into a medium size saucepan.

Reduce the sauce, over high heat, for 4 to 5 minutes.

Strain the sauce.

Skim off as much of the fat as possible.

Carve the roast and pour the meat drippings into the sauce.

Serve the sauce and the roast beef separately.

119
Club Steak Bordelaise

For 2 people

---

2 10 OUNCE CLUB STEAKS, DEBONED
1 TABLESPOON VEGETABLE OIL
   SALT
   FRESHLY GROUND PEPPER
1 CUP HOT BOURGUIGNON SAUCE [*Recipe 30*]
1 TEASPOON FRESH PARSLEY, FINELY CHOPPED

Place the vegetable oil in a very thick sauté pan, over high heat.

When the oil begins to smoke, discard the oil.
Reduce the heat to medium and immediately add the steaks.

Cook the steaks for:

5 minutes on each side: *medium rare*
6 minutes on each side: *medium*
8 minutes on each side: *well done*

Season the steaks with salt and pepper and transfer them to a heated serving platter.

Pour the sauce over the steaks.

Garnish with the chopped parsley.

120
Steak, Chinese Style

For 2 people

---

2 ½ POUND STEAKS, CLUB STEAKS OR
   FILET MIGNON
3 TABLESPOONS BUTTER
   SALT
   FRESHLY GROUND PEPPER
1 SMALL ONION, THINLY SLICED
½ GREEN PEPPER, SEEDED AND THINLY SLICED
12 MUSHROOMS, SLICED
1 GARLIC CLOVE, SMASHED AND FINELY CHOPPED
   TOMATO, CUT INTO 4 WEDGES

Cut the steaks into thin slices, at an angle.

In a sauté pan, melt 2 tablespoons butter over high heat.
As soon as the foam subsides add the steak.
Reduce the heat to medium and cook, uncovered, for 3 minutes on each side.
Season the steaks with salt and pepper and transfer to a heated platter.

Melt 1 tablespoon of butter in the sauté pan.
As soon as the butter begins to foam, add the onion, and cook, uncovered, for one minute.
Add the green pepper to the onion and cook for one minute, stirring occasionally.
Add the sliced mushrooms and the garlic and cook for 3 minutes, stirring occasionally.
Add the tomato wedges and cook for another 1 to 2 minutes.
Season the vegetables to taste with salt and pepper.

Mix the steak and beef drippings into the vegetables and arrange on a bed of rice.

Serve immediately.

121
Club Steak au Poivre
For 2 people

---

2 10 OUNCE CLUB STEAKS, DEBONED
1 TABLESPOON PEPPERCORNS, COARSLEY SMASHED
1 TABLESPOON CLARIFIED BUTTER
3 TABLESPOONS COGNAC
½ CUP HOT BROWN SAUCE THIN [*Recipe 28*] OR
    ½ CUP ROAST BEEF DRIPPINGS
½ CUP HEAVY CREAM
  SALT
  FRESHLY GROUND PEPPER
1 TEASPOON CHOPPED PARSLEY

Press the smashed peppercorns into the steaks.

Melt the clarified butter in a thick sauté pan, over high heat,
When the butter is hot, add the steaks.
Reduce the heat to medium and cook the steaks for:

5 minutes on each side: *medium rare*
6 minutes on each side: *medium*
7 minutes on each side: *well done*

Remove the sauté pan from the heat and let cool for a few minutes.

Pour in the cognac and set the cognac alight with a match.
After the flame has died, transfer the steaks to a heated serving platter.

Pour the sauce (or roast beef drippings) into the sauté pan.
Bring to a boil over high heat.
Reduce the heat to medium, add the cream and simmer for 2 to 3 minutes.
Season the sauce to taste with salt and pepper.

Pour the drippings from the steaks into the sauce.

Garnish with chopped parsley.

122
Club Steak à la Halna

For 4 people

---

4 ¾ POUND CLUB STEAKS
1½ TABLESPOONS PEPPERCORNS, COARSLEY SMASHED
3 TABLESPOONS CLARIFIED BUTTER
3 OUNCES COGNAC
SALT
2 TABLESPOONS BUTTER
2 DRIED SHALLOTS, FINELY CHOPPED

Press the crushed peppercorns into the steaks.

Melt the clarified butter in a thick sauté pan, over high heat,
When the butter is hot, add the steaks.
Reduce the heat to medium and cook the steaks for:

5 minutes on each side: *medium rare*
6 minutes on each side: *medium*
7 minutes on each side: *well done*

Remove the sauté pan from the heat and let cool for a few minutes.

Pour in the cognac and set the cognac alight with a match.

After the flame has died, transfer the steaks to a heated serving platter. Season the steaks with salt.

Melt 2 tablespoons fresh butter in the sauté pan.

Add the dried shallots and cook for one minute, over medium heat.
Pour this sauce over the steaks.

123
Top Round Strogonoff

For 4 people

1½ POUNDS TOP ROUND, CUT INTO THIN STRIPS AT
    AN ANGLE
6 TABLESPOONS CLARIFIED BUTTER
2 SMALL ONIONS, THINLY SLICED
½ POUND MUSHROOMS, SLICED
1 TEASPOON PAPRIKA
¾ TEASPOON TOMATO PASTE
4 TABLESPOONS HOT BASIC BROWN SAUCE, THIN
    [*Recipe 28*] OR
    4 TABLESPOONS BEEF DRIPPINGS
½ CUP SOUR CREAM
    SALT
    FRESHLY GROUND PEPPER
    JUICE OF ½ LEMON
    DASH OF CAYENNE PEPPER
1 TABLESPOON FRESH PARSLEY, FINELY CHOPPED

In a sauté pan, melt 3 tablespoons clarified butter over high heat.

When the butter is hot, add the onions, reduce the heat to low, cover and cook for 8 to 10 minutes, stirring occasionally. Add the mushrooms and cook, uncovered, for 5 minutes, stirring occasionally.

Mix in the paprika, the sauce (or beef drippings), the tomato paste and the sour cream. Season the sauce to taste.

Remove the sauté pan from the heat and set aside.

In a separate sauté pan, melt the remaining clarified butter over high heat.

When the butter is hot, add the beef and sauté, over high heat, for 3 minutes.

Season the beef and mix it into the sauce.
Squeeze in the lemon juice and add the cayenne pepper.

Sprinkle with fresh parsley.

Serve the Beef Strogonoff with egg noodles.

124
Braised Short Ribs
For 4 people

3½ POUNDS SHORT RIBS
    MARINADE [RECIPE 1]
½ POUND SALT PORK, DICED
2 ONIONS, PEELED AND CUT INTO 4
1 CARROT, CUT INTO 1" PIECES
1 CELERY BRANCH, CUT INTO 1" PIECES
    BAY LEAF
    PINCH OF THYME
½ TEASPOON OREGANO
2 CUPS HOT BASIC BROWN SAUCE THIN [*Recipe 28*]
    SALT
    FRESHLY GROUND PEPPER

AHEAD OF TIME: Cover the short ribs with marinade. Cover with wax paper. Refrigerate and marinate the ribs for 24 hours.

Preheat the oven to 350°.

Remove the ribs from the marinade and pat the ribs dry with paper towels.
Strain the marinade into a saucepan.
Bring the strained marinade to a boil and reduce the liquid by two thirds, over high heat.

In a large, ovenproof casserole, sauté the salt pork over high heat, for 4 minutes.
Add the short ribs and sauté, uncovered, for 5 to 6 minutes,

or until the short ribs are brown on each side.
Add the vegetables and the herbs and sauté for 4 to 5 minutes.

Pour the brown sauce and then the reduced marinade, over the ribs.
Season to taste with salt and pepper.
Bring the sauce to a boil over high heat.
Cover the casserole and place in the oven for 1½ hours.

125
Boeuf Bourguignon

For 4 people

---

3 POUNDS BLADE STEAK
MARINADE [RECIPE 1]
2 TABLESPOONS VEGETABLE OIL
1 TABLESPOON BUTTER
SALT
FRESHLY GROUND PEPPER
A BAY LEAF
½ TEASPOON CHERVIL
¼ TEASPOON THYME
½ TEASPOON TARRAGON
3 GARLIC CLOVES, SMASHED AND FINELY CHOPPED
2 DRIED SHALLOTS, FINELY CHOPPED
4 TABLESPOONS FLOUR
2½ CUPS HOT BASIC BROWN STOCK [*Recipe 15 or 16*]
8 OUNCES SALTED PORK, DICED
18 WHITE ONIONS, PEELED
½ POUND MUSHROOMS, CUT IN 2
1 TABLESPOON FRESH PARSLEY, FINELY CHOPPED

AHEAD OF TIME: Trim the blade steak and cut it into 1½" cubes.
Cover the beef with marinade. Cover with wax paper.
Refrigerate and marinate the beef for at least 12 hours.

Preheat the oven to 350°.

Dry the beef with paper towels.

Strain the marinade into a saucepan and reduce it by two thirds, over high heat. Set aside.

Place the vegetable oil and the butter over high heat, in a large heavy ovenproof casserole.

As soon as the foam subsides, add the beef, a few pieces at a time and brown the meat, uncovered, over high heat.

Season the meat with salt and pepper.

Add the herbs, the garlic and the dried shallots and reduce the heat to medium. Simmer the seasonings for one minute.

Add the flour and cook the roux, uncovered, for 4 to 5 minutes, stirring constantly.

Remove the casserole from the heat.

Add one cup of beef stock into the roux and mix in thoroughly with a wooden spoon.

Return the casserole to the top of the stove, over low heat.

Add the remaining beef stock, one cup at a time, while stirring constantly.

Stir in the reduced marinade.

Season the sauce with salt and pepper.

Bring the sauce to a boil over high heat.

Cover the casserole and place it in the oven for one hour.

Sauté the pork for 3 to 4 minutes, over high heat, in a sauté pan.

Add the onions to the pork, reduce the heat to medium and cook, uncovered, for 4 minutes.

Add the mushrooms and cook, uncovered, for 4 minutes.

Season.

Add to the Boeuf Bourguignon.

Cover the casserole and return it to the oven for one-half hour.

Garnish the Boeuf Bourguignon with chopped parsley and serve from the casserole.

126
Stuffed Beef Flank

For 4 people

---

          2   I POUND FLANKS
              SALT
              FRESHLY GROUND PEPPER
          I   CUP STUFFING [RECIPE 6]
          I   TABLESPOON VEGETABLE OIL
        2½   TABLESPOONS BUTTER
          2   TABLESPOONS CARROTS, CHOPPED
          2   TABLESPOONS ONIONS, CHOPPED
          I   TABLESPOON CELERY, CHOPPED
              A BAY LEAF
         ¼   TEASPOON BASIL
              A PINCH OF THYME
          I   GARLIC CLOVE SMASHED AND FINELY CHOPPED
          3   TABLESPOONS FLOUR
        I½   CUPS HOT BASIC BROWN BEEF STOCK [*Recipe 15 or 16*]
          4   TOMATOES, CUT INTO 4 WEDGES OR
                  I½ CUPS CANNED TOMATOES, DRAINED AND
                  COARSLEY CHOPPED

Preheat the oven to 350°.

Slit flanks in two lengthwise, stopping ¼" from one edge.
Open the flank and place it flat on a wooden chopping board.
Pound the flank with a cleaver.

Season the flanks and fill each flank with one half of the stuffing.
Roll the flanks and secure with kitchen string.

Place 1 tablespoon vegetable oil in a sauté pan, over high heat.
When the oil is hot, add the rolled flanks. When the flanks are
brown on both sides, transfer them to an ovenproof casserole.
Season the flanks with salt and pepper.

Melt 2 tablespoons butter in the sauté pan, over high heat, until it begins to foam.

Add the chopped carrots, onions, celery, herbs and garlic; reduce the heat to medium and cook, uncovered, for 4 to 5 minutes, stirring occasionally.

Add the flour to the vegetables and cook, uncovered, over low heat, for 6 minutes, while stirring constantly.

Remove the pan from the heat. Add one cup of beef stock into the "roux" and mix in thoroughly with a wooden spoon. Return the pan to the top of the stove, over low heat. Add the remaining beef stock, stir and bring the sauce to a boil.

In a separate sauté pan, melt the remaining butter over high heat, until it begins to foam. Add the tomatoes and cook, uncovered, for one to two minutes, stirring frequently.

Pour the tomatoes and the sauce over the flanks.

Season the sauce to taste, cover the casserole and place it in the oven for 1½ hours.

Strain the sauce before serving.

127
Stuffed Cabbage Rolls

For 4 people

 I LARGE CABBAGE
 2 TABLESPOONS BUTTER
 I DRIED SHALLOT, FINELY CHOPPED
 I GARLIC CLOVE, SMASHED AND FINELY CHOPPED
 I TABLESPOON FRESH PARSLEY, FINELY CHOPPED
 I ONION, PEELED AND FINELY CHOPPED
 2 APPLES, PEELED, CORED AND FINELY CHOPPED
 I POUND LEAN MINCED BEEF
   SALT

FRESHLY GROUND PEPPER
¼ CUP BREADCRUMBS
1 BEATEN EGG
2 CUPS HOT QUICK TOMATO SAUCE [*Recipe 33*]

Preheat the oven to 375°.

Drop the cabbage into a stockpot three-quarters filled with boiling, salted water.
Blanch the cabbage for 4 minutes.
Cool the cabbage under running water, for at least 4 minutes.
Carefully remove 8 large leaves from the cabbage, drain the leaves and set them aside.

In a sauté pan, melt the butter over high heat, until it begins to foam.
Reduce the heat to medium, add the chopped shallots, the garlic, the parsley, the onion and the apple; cook, uncovered, for 4 minutes, stirring occasionally.
Add the minced beef and cook, uncovered, for 5 to 6 minutes, stirring occasionally.
Season the mixture with salt and pepper.
Remove the sauté pan from the heat and mix the breadcrumbs and the beaten egg into the stuffing.
Correct the seasonings.

Place an equal amount of stuffing in each of the reserved cabbage leaves.

Roll the cabbage leaf over the meat stuffing. As you roll the cabbage leaf, tuck in the edges towards the middle. Secure the rolls with a toothpick.

Arrange the cabbage rolls in a buttered baking dish.
Pour the tomato sauce over the rolls.
Cover the baking dish and place in the oven for 25 minutes.

Before serving, discard the toothpicks.

128
Brochettes of Beef

For 4 people

1½ POUNDS BEEF TENDERLOIN, CUT INTO 1½" CUBES
   MARINADE [*Recipe 1*]
1 ITALIAN ONION, CUT INTO 1" PIECES
8 SLICES BACON, CUT INTO 3 PIECES
20 MUSHROOM CAPS
   SALT
   FRESHLY GROUND PEPPER
2 TABLESPOONS GARLIC BUTTER [*Recipe 8*]

AHEAD OF TIME: Cover the beef with marinade. Cover with wax paper.
Refrigerate the beef and marinate for at least 12 hours.

On a skewer, alternate the beef, onions, bacon and mushroom caps.
Season the brochettes with salt and pepper.

Broil, 6" away from the broiling element, or barbecue, for

   4 minutes: *medium rare*
  12 minutes: *well done*

Baste the brochettes occasionally with the marinade.

When the brochettes are almost done, spread ½ tablespoon of garlic butter on each brochette.
Return the brochettes to the oven (or barbecue) and melt the garlic butter.

Serve with rice.

Chicken

129
Coq au Vin

For 4 people

---

3 POUND CHICKEN, CUT INTO 8 PIECES
1 CUP FLOUR
3 TABLESPOONS CLARIFIED BUTTER
3 OUNCES LEAN PORK, DICED
   SALT
   FRESHLY GROUND PEPPER
4 TABLESPOONS COGNAC [OPTIONAL]
2 DRIED SHALLOTS, FINELY CHOPPED
2 GARLIC CLOVES, SMASHED AND FINELY CHOPPED
1 CUP DRY RED OR WHITE WINE
1½ CUPS HOT BASIC BROWN SAUCE THIN [*Recipe 28*]
BOUQUET GARNI CONSISTING OF
   ¼ TEASPOON THYME
      BAY LEAF
   ¼ TEASPOON ROSEMARY
   ¼ TEASPOON BASIL
   ½ TEASPOON CHERVIL
      FRESH PARSLEY
      CELERY [*See basic brown beef stock 2, Recipe 16*]
1 TABLESPOON BUTTER
15 SMALL WHITE ONIONS, PEELED
½ POUND MUSHROOMS, CUT INTO 4
1 TABLESPOON FRESH PARSLEY, FINELY CHOPPED

Preheat the oven to 350°.

Wash the chicken pieces under cold running water and dry

thoroughly with paper towels. Dip them in flour and gently shake off the excess flour.

In a sauté pan, melt the clarified butter over high heat.
When the butter is hot, reduce the heat to medium, add the chicken pieces and the diced pork and cook, uncovered, for 8 minutes on each side, or until the chicken becomes golden brown.
Season with salt and pepper.

Transfer the chicken pieces and the pork to a heavy, ovenproof casserole. Bring the cognac to the boiling point, over the heat, and pour the cognac over the chicken.
Set the cognac alight with a match.

Add the shallots and the garlic to the sauté pan, and cook over medium heat, for one minute, stirring constantly.
Pour in the wine and increase the heat to high.
Reduce the wine by one half.

Pour the reduced wine and the brown sauce over the chicken.
Add the bouquet garni.
Season the sauce with salt and pepper.

Place the casserole over high heat and bring the sauce to a boil, on top of the stove.

Cover and place the casserole in the oven for 30 minutes.

In the sauté pan, melt 1 tablespoon butter over high heat, until it begins to foam. Add the onions, reduce the heat to medium and cook, uncovered, for 2 minutes, stirring occasionally.
Add the mushrooms to the onions and simmer, uncovered, for 5 minutes, stirring occasionally.
Season with salt and pepper.

Add the onions and mushrooms to the Coq au Vin.
Correct the seasonings.
Cover and return the casserole to the oven for 15 minutes.

Discard the bouquet garni.

Sprinkle the Coq au Vin with chopped parsley.
Serve from the casserole.

130
Chicken Casserole
For 4 people

---

3 POUND CHICKEN, CUT INTO 8 PIECES
1 CUP FLOUR
   SALT
   FRESHLY GROUND PEPPER
3 TABLESPOONS CLARIFIED BUTTER
1 DRIED SHALLOT FINELY CHOPPED
½ POUND MUSHROOMS, CUT IN 4
1 CUP CARROTS, CUT INTO THIN STRIPS
15 SMALL WHITE ONIONS, PEELED
½ CUP HOT BASIC CHICKEN STOCK [*Recipe 17 or 18*]
½ TEASPOON OREGANO

Preheat the oven to 350°.

Drop the carrots into a large saucepan filled with boiling, salted water. Blanch the carrots for 7 minutes.
Remove the saucepan from the heat. Cool the carrots under running water for at least 4 minutes.
Drain and set aside.

Wash the chicken pieces under cold, running water. Dry them thoroughly with paper towels.

Season the chicken pieces with salt and pepper and dip them in flour. Shake off the excess flour.
In a sauté pan, melt the clarified butter over high heat.
When the butter is hot, add the chicken pieces, reduce the heat to medium and cook, uncovered, for 8 minutes on each side, or until they become golden brown. Add the vegetables and cook, un-

covered, for 1 to 2 minutes.
Transfer the chicken and the vegetables to an ovenproof casserole.

Pour the chicken stock over the chicken and add the oregano.
Season to taste with salt and pepper.
Cover and place in the oven, for 45 minutes.
Correct the seasonings.
Serve the chicken from the casserole.

131
Chicken Kiev

For 4 people

---

    2 LARGE CHICKEN BREASTS
      SALT
      FRESHLY GROUND PEPPER
  ½ CUP GARLIC BUTTER, FROZEN [*Recipe 8*]
    3 EGGS
    1 TABLESPOON VEGETABLE OIL
    1 CUP FLOUR
    2 CUPS BREADCRUMBS

      PEANUT OIL, IN A DEEP FRYER, HEATED
        TO 325°

Debone and skin the chicken breasts and wash them under cold running water.
Split each chicken breast in two, lengthwise.

One by one, place each piece of chicken between 2 pieces of aluminium foil and flatten them with a cleaver.

Season the flattened chicken pieces with salt and pepper.
Place 1 tablespoon of garlic butter at one end of the flattened chicken piece and roll the chicken over the garlic butter.

As you roll the chicken, tuck in the edges towards the middle. Secure the rolls with a toothpick.

Beat the eggs and vegetable oil together.

Dip the chicken rolls, one at a time, first in the flour, then in the beaten eggs and then in the breadcrumbs.

Deepfry the rolls in peanut oil, until golden brown.

Serve with quick tomato sauce (Recipe 33)

132
Chicken Arlesienne

For 4 people

---

3 POUND CHICKEN, CUT INTO 8 PIECES
1 CUP FLOUR
  SALT
  FRESHLY GROUND PEPPER
2 TABLESPOONS VEGETABLE OIL
1 ONION, PEELED AND THINLY SLICED
1 GARLIC CLOVE, SMASHED AND FINELY CHOPPED
½ TEASPOON TARRAGON
½ CUP DRY WHITE WINE
3 TOMATOES, PEELED AND CUT INTO 4 WEDGES
½ SMALL EGGPLANT, PEELED AND THINLY SLICED

Preheat the oven to 350°.

Wash the chicken pieces under cold running water. Dry them thoroughly with paper towels.

Season the chicken pieces with salt and pepper and dip them in flour. Shake off the excess flour.

Place the vegetable oil in a sauté pan with an ovenproof or

metal handle, over high heat. When the oil is hot, add the chicken pieces and cook, uncovered, for 8 minutes on each side, or until golden brown.

Add the onions, garlic and tarragon to the chicken and cook, uncovered, for 2 minutes.
Pour the wine over the chicken. Increase the heat to high, and reduce the liquid by one half.

Add the tomatoes and the eggplant to the chicken.
Season with salt and pepper. Cover.
Place in the oven for 45 minutes.

133
Chicken New Orleans

For 4 people

---

3 POUND CHICKEN, CUT INTO 8 PIECES
SALT
FRESHLY GROUND PEPPER
3 EGGS
1 TABLESPOON VEGETABLE OIL
1½ CUPS FLOUR
1½ CUPS BREADCRUMBS
2 BANANAS
PEANUT OIL, IN A DEEP FRYER, HEATED
TO 325°

Preheat the oven to 400°.

Wash the chicken pieces under cold running water.
Drain the chicken pieces on paper towels.

In a mixing bowl, beat the eggs and vegetable oil together.

Season the chicken pieces with salt and pepper.

Dip each chicken piece into the flour, into the beaten eggs and then into the breadcrumbs.

Deepfry the chicken pieces until deep golden brown.

Drain the chicken pieces on paper towels and then transfer them to a baking dish.

Place the chicken pieces in the oven for 8 to 10 minutes.

Peel the bananas, cut them in two and then split each half, lengthwise.

Dip the banana slices into the flour, into the beaten eggs and then into the breadcrumbs.

Deepfry the banana slices until golden.

Serve the deepfried chicken and banana slices together, on a heated serving platter.

134
Everyday Chicken

For 4 people

---

3 POUND CHICKEN, CUT INTO 8 PIECES
1 CUP FLOUR
  SALT
  FRESHLY GROUND PEPPER
3 TABLESPOONS CLARIFIED BUTTER
1 ONION, VERY COARSELY DICED
1 GREEN PEPPER, VERY COARSELY DICED
  PINCH THYME
1 GARLIC CLOVE, SMASHED AND FINELY CHOPPED
4 TOMATOES, PEELED AND CUT INTO 4 WEDGES

Wash the chicken under cold running water.
Dry the chicken thoroughly with paper towels.

Dip the chicken pieces in the flour and shake off the excess flour.
Season the chicken pieces with salt and pepper.

Melt the clarified butter in a sauté pan, over high heat.
When the butter is hot, add the chicken and brown, uncovered,
for 8 minutes on each side.

Add the remaining ingredients to the chicken and season with
salt and pepper.

Cover, reduce the heat to very low and cook for 30 minutes.
Stir occasionally.

135
Chicken à la Point

For 4 people

---

3 POUND CHICKEN
SALT
FRESHLY GROUND WHITE PEPPER
5 TABLESPOONS UNSALTED [SWEET] BUTTER
¼ CUP COGNAC
½ CUP PORT WINE
1½ CUPS HEAVY CREAM
1 TEASPOON TARRAGON
1 TEASPOON KNEADED BUTTER [MANIÉ BUTTER]
    [RECIPE 12]
1 TABLESPOON FRESH PARSLEY, FINELY CHOPPED

Preheat the oven to 300°.

Wash the chicken under cold running water.
Thoroughly dry the chicken both inside and out, with paper
towels.
Season the main cavity and the outside of the chicken with
salt and pepper.

In a heavy, ovenproof casserole, melt the butter over low heat. As soon as the butter has melted, place the chicken in the casserole, cover and place in the oven for 1½ hours.
The chicken is done when it is nearly white.

Transfer the chicken to a carving board.
Discard the fat which has formed in the casserole and reserve the drippings.
Place the casserole on top of the stove and add the cognac to the cooking liquor. Set the cognac alight with a match. Add the port wine and reduce the wine over high heat, for 2 minutes.
Pour in the cream, add the tarragon and season to taste with salt and pepper. Bring the liquid to a boil. Cook for 2 minutes.
Whisk the kneaded butter into the boiling liquid.

Carve the chicken and arrange on a heated serving platter.
Pour any drippings into the white sauce.
Pour the sauce over the chicken.
Sprinkle with chopped parsley.

136
Roast Chicken

For 4 people

---

3 POUND CHICKEN
SALT
FRESHLY GROUND PEPPER
4 TABLESPOONS BUTTER AT ROOM TEMPERATURE
2 TABLESPOONS CARROTS, DICED
2 TABLESPOONS ONIONS, DICED
1 TABLESPOON CELERY, DICED
½ TEASPOON CHERVIL
½ TEASPOON FRESH PARSLEY, FINELY CHOPPED
1½ CUPS HOT BASIC CHICKEN STOCK [*Recipe 17 or 18*]

Preheat oven to 400°.

Wash the chicken under cold, running water.
Thoroughly dry the chicken, both inside and out, with paper towels.
Season the main cavity of the chicken with salt and pepper.
Place 1 tablespoon of butter inside the main cavity of the chicken.
Truss the chicken with white kitchen string.

Spread the remaining butter over the outside of the chicken and season with salt and pepper.

Place the chicken on a rack, in a roasting pan.
After the chicken has been in the oven for 15 to 20 minutes, reduce the oven heat to 350°. Baste the chicken occasionally.

Roast the chicken for 60 to 70 minutes and then transfer it to a heated serving platter.

Add the vegetables and the chervil to the fat in the roasting pan and cook over medium heat, uncovered, for 3 minutes, on top of the stove.
Add the chicken stock to the vegetables and season the sauce with salt and pepper.
Pour the contents of the roasting pan into a medium size saucepan. Bring the sauce to a boil over high heat and boil briskly for 4 to 5 minutes.
Strain the sauce.
Skim off as much surface fat as possible.

Serve the sauce and the chicken separately.

Duck

137
Duck à la Stanley Park

For 2 people

1	3-POUND DUCK
7	ORANGES
2	LEMONS
	SALT
	FRESHLY GROUND PEPPER
2	TABLESPOONS DICED CARROTS
2	TABLESPOONS DICED ONION
1	TABLESPOON DICED CELERY
	BAY LEAF
	PINCH THYME
¼	TEASPOON BASIL
2	CUPS DRY RED WINE
2	CUPS HOT BASIC BROWN SAUCE THIN [*Recipe 28*]
½	CUP SUGAR
3	TABLESPOONS WHITE VINEGAR
½	CUP CURAÇAO
1	TEASPOON CORNSTARCH

Preheat the oven to 425°.

Trim off the excess fat from the duck.
Wash the duck under cold running water.
Thoroughly dry the duck, both inside and out, with paper towels.

Rub the outside of the duck with 2 oranges, cut in two.
Save the oranges for other use, if desired.

Season the main cavity of the duck with salt and pepper.

Cut an orange and a lemon into four wedges each and place the wedges inside the main cavity of the duck.

Truss the duck with white kitchen tring.

Place the duck on a rack in a roasting pan.

Brown the duck in the oven for 30 minutes.

Squeeze the juice of an orange over the duck.

Reduce the oven heat to 350° and roast the duck for 1½ hours.

Pierce the thigh with a fork. If no trace of blood is apparent, the duck is cooked.

Set the duck aside on a heated platter.

Discard two-thirds of the fat in the roasting pan.

Place the roasting pan on top of the stove, over medium heat.

Add the diced vegetables and the herbs to the duck fat and cook, uncovered, for 5 minutes.

Add the red wine to the vegetables, increase the heat to high and reduce the liquid by two thirds.

Add the brown sauce and season to taste with salt and pepper.

Bring the sauce to a boil and simmer for 2 minutes over low heat.

In a separate saucepan, place the sugar and the white vinegar over high heat.

Bring the mixture to a boil and reduce the heat to medium.

As soon as the sugar-vinegar mixture becomes dark brown, remove the saucepan from the heat.

Add the juice of 2 oranges and return to the top of the stove.

When the mixture becomes iquid, pour it into the brown sauce.

Strain the sauce.

In a small dish, dissolve the cornstarch in the curaçao, and mix into the sauce.

Remove the rind from one orange and one lemon.

Plunge the rind into a saucepan three-quarters filled with boiling

water, and blanch for 3 to 4 minutes.
Drain the rind on paper towels.

Carve the duck and arrange on a heated serving platter.
Pour any drippings from the duck into the sauce.
Pour the sauce over the duck.
Garnish with the blanched orange and lemon rinds.

Lamb

138
Lamb Shish Kebabs

For 4 people

1½ POUND LOIN OF LAMB CUT INTO 1½" CUBES
   MARINADE [RECIPE 3]
8 BAY LEAVES
2 LARGE ONIONS, CUT INTO 4
½ POUND CHERRY TOMATOES
20 MUSHROOM CAPS

AHEAD OF TIME: Cover the lamb cubes with marinade.
Cover with wax paper. Refrigerate, and marinate the lamb for 8 hours.

Preheat the oven to Broil.

Remove the lamb cubes from the marinade.
Alternate the lamb cubes, and the remaining ingredients, on 4 skewers.

Broil, or barbecue, the shish kebabs for 12 to 15 minutes.
Baste occasionally with the marinade.

Serve the shish-kebabs with rice pilaf (Recipe 156).

Pork

139
Roast Loin of Pork

For 4 people

---

3 POUND LOIN OF PORK, DEBONED*
2 GARLIC CLOVES, PEELED AND CUT INTO 4 SLIVERS
   EACH
   SALT
   FRESHLY GROUND PEPPER
2 TABLESPOONS VEGETABLE OIL
6 APPLES
1 TABLESPOON DICED CARROTS
1 TABLESPOON DICED ONIONS
1 TABLESPOON DICED CELERY
   PINCH THYME
½ TEASPOON ROSEMARY
½ CUP HOT BASIC CHICKEN STOCK [*Recipe 17 or 18*)

Preheat the oven to 425°.

With a paring knife, make small incisions in the loin of pork and insert the slivers of garlic.

Season the loin of pork with salt and pepper.
Pour the vegetable oil into the roasting pan, and place the roasting pan in the oven for 4 to 5 minutes, or until the oil is hot.
Place the loin of pork, and the reserved bones, beside one another, in the roasting pan.
Return the roasting pan to the oven for 20 minutes at 425°.

Reduce the oven heat to 350°.

Total roasting time, including 20 minutes at 425°: 30 minutes per pound.

Discard the fat every 15 minutes.
Remove the roasting pan from the oven and transfer the roast to a carving board. Leave the pork bones in the pan.
Discard all but 2 tablespoons of fat from the roasting pan.
While the juices of the roast are settling, peel and core the apples, and cut each apple into 4.
Add the apples, the diced vegetables and the herbs to the fat in the roasting pan.
Place the roasting pan on top of the stove, over medium-high heat and cook, uncovered, for 4 to 5 minutes.
Discard the bone and pour in the chicken stock.
Season the sauce with salt and pepper and add any drippings from the roast.
Skim off as much of the fat as possible.
Carve the roast, and pour the sauce over the roast pork slices.

*Ask your butcher to debone the loin of pork.
 Reserve the bones.

140
Stuffed Pork Tenderloin

For 4 people

---

  2 ONE-POUND PORK TENDERLOINS, TRIMMED
    SALT
    FRESHLY GROUND PEPPER
 ½ CUP STUFFING [RECIPE 6]
  2 TABLESPOONS BUTTER
  I TABLESPOON CHOPPED CARROTS
  I TABLESPOON CHOPPED ONIONS
  I TABLESPOON CHOPPED CELERY
    PINCH THYME
 ¼ TEASPOON OREGANO

2 TABLESPOONS FLOUR

2 CUPS HOT BASIC CHICKEN STOCK [*Recipe 17 or 18*]

Preheat the oven to 350°.

Slit the tenderloin lengthwise to a depth of three-quarters of the thickness.
Season and place one half of the stuffing inside each tenderloin.
Secure with white kitchen string.

In a small roasting pan, melt the butter over high heat until the foam subsides.
Immediately add the stuffed tenderloins, reduce the heat to medium and brown the tenderloins on both sides, uncovered.
Transfer the tenderloins to a heated platter.
Add the chopped vegetables and the herbs to the roasting pan and cook, uncovered, for 2 to 3 minutes.
Add the flour and cook the "roux" for 4 to 5 minutes, stirring constantly.
Remove the roasting pan from the heat.
Add one cup of chicken stock to the "roux" and mix in thoroughly with a wooden spoon.
Return the pan to the top of the stove, over low heat.
Pour in the remaining stock, while stirring constantly.
Bring the sauce to a boil.
Return the pork tenderloins to the roasting pan.
Season with salt and pepper.

Cover the pan and place in the oven for 45 minutes.

141
Pork Chops à la Diable

For 4 people

---

8 PORK CHOPS 1″ THICK
2 TABLESPOONS VEGETABLE OIL
 SALT
 FRESHLY GROUND PEPPER
1½ CUPS HOT DEVILLED SAUCE [RECIPE 31]
1 LARGE DILL PICKLE, CUT INTO THIN STRIPS
1 TABLESPOON FRESH PARSLEY, FINELY CHOPPED

Preheat the oven to 300°.

Trim off most of the fat from the pork chops.

Place the vegetable oil in a sauté pan with an ovenproof or metal handle over high heat.
When the oil is hot, add the pork chops, reduce the heat to medium and brown the pork chops, uncovered, for 7 minutes on each side.
Occasionally remove the fat from the pan while the pork chops are browning.
Season the pork chops with salt and pepper.
Transfer the sauté pan to the oven and continue to cook the pork chops for 5 to 6 minutes.

Remove the sauté pan from the oven and transfer the pork chops to a heated serving platter.

Discard the fat from the sauté pan.
Pour in the devilled sauce and add the pickles and the parsley.
Bring the sauce to a boil and simmer, uncovered, over medium heat, for 2 minutes.

Pour the sauce over the pork chops.

Veal

142
Veal Scaloppine Printanière

For 4 people

1¾ POUNDS VEAL SCALLOPS, CUT INTO 1½"
    SQUARES ⅜" THICK
½ CUP CARROTS, CUT INTO THIN STRIPS
1 CUP FLOUR
  SALT
  FRESHLY GROUND PEPPER
3 TABLESPOONS CLARIFIED BUTTER
12 WHITE ONIONS, PEELED
½ CUP MUSHROOMS CUT INTO 4
  WATER CHESTNUT, THINLY SLICED
½ TEASPOON OREGANO
½ CUP DRY WHITE WINE
½ CUP HOT BASIC CHICKEN STOCK [*Recipe 17 or 18*]
1 TABLESPOON FRESH PARSLEY, FINELY CHOPPED

Drop the carrots into a large saucepan half-filled with boiling, salted water.
Blanch the carrots for 7 minutes.
Cool the carrots under running water for at least 5 minutes.
Drain and set aside.

Dip the pieces of veal into flour and gently shake off the excess.
flour.
Season the veal with salt and pepper.

In a sauté pan, melt the clarified butter over high heat.
Add the veal and sauté, uncovered, for 3 minutes on each side.

Transfer the veal to a heated serving platter.

Reduce the heat under the sauté pan to medium.
Add the onions and cook, uncovered, for 2 minutes.
Add the blanched carrots, the mushrooms, the water chestnut and the oregano. Cook, uncovered, for 2 to 3 minutes, stirring occasionally.
Pour in the white wine and bring the liquid to a boil over high heat. Reduce the liquid by two thirds over high heat.
Add the chicken stock and boil briskly for 5 to 6 minutes.
Season the sauce and add the chopped parsley.

Pour the sauce over the veal scallops.

143
Veal Chops with Artichoke Hearts

For 2 people

---

4 8-OUNCE VEAL CHOPS
1 CUP FLOUR
   SALT
   FRESHLY GROUND PEPPER
3 TABLESPOONS CLARIFIED BUTTER
4 CANNED ARTICHOKE HEARTS, DRAINED AND CUT IN TWO
1 DRIED SHALLOT, FINELY CHOPPED
½ CUP HOT BASIC CHICKEN STOCK *(Recipe 17 or 18)*
1 TEASPOON FRESH PARSLEY, FINELY CHOPPED

Dip the veal chops in flour and shake off the excess flour.
Season the veal chops with salt and pepper.

In a sauté pan, melt the clarified butter over high heat.
When the butter is hot, add the veal chops, reduce the heat to medium and cook, uncovered, for 6 minutes on each side.

Add the artichoke hearts and cook for 2 to 3 minutes.
Season the veal chops with salt and pepper.
Transfer the veal chops and artichoke hearts to a heated platter.

Add the chopped shallots to the sauté pan and cook for one minute.
Pour in the chicken stock and reduce the liquid over high heat.
Add the chopped parsley, and season.
Pour the sauce over the veal chops and artichokes.

144
Blanquette of Veal

For 4 people

---

2 POUNDS SHOULDER OF VEAL, CUT INTO 1½" CUBES
1 ONION, STUDDED WITH 2 WHOLE CLOVES
2 CARROTS, PEELED
1 LEEK, CLEANED
BOUQUET GARNI CONSISTING OF
½ TEASPOON THYME
   BAY LEAF
½ TEASPOON TARRAGON
½ TEASPOON CHERVIL
   FRESH PARSLEY
   CELERY [*See basic brown beef stock 2, Recipe 16*]
3 CUPS HOT BASIC CHICKEN STOCK [*Recipe 17 or 18*]
6 TABLESPOONS BUTTER
24 WHITE ONIONS, PEELED
½ POUND MUSHROOMS, CUT INTO 4
4 TABLESPOONS FLOUR
1 EGG YOLK
2 TABLESPOONS HEAVY CREAM

1 TABLESPOON FRESH PARSLEY, FINELY CHOPPED
SALT
FRESHLY GROUND PEPPER

Place the veal in a large saucepan and cover the veal with cold water.
Bring the liquid to a boil over high heat.
Skim and then strain the meat.

Transfer the meat to another large saucepan.
Add the onion studded with cloves, the carrots, the leek, the bouquet garni and the chicken stock.
If necessary, add water to cover.
Season with salt and pepper.
Bring the liquid to a boil over high heat.
Reduce the heat to medium and simmer, uncovered, for one hour.

In a sauté pan, melt 2 tablespoons butter over high heat, until it begins to foam.
Add the white onions, reduce the heat to medium and cook, uncovered, for 2 minutes, stirring occasionally.
Add the mushrooms and cook, uncovered, for 2 to 3 minutes, stirring occasionally.
Season with salt and pepper.

Add the onions and mushrooms to the veal and simmer, uncovered, for 15 minutes.

Discard the onion studded with cloves, the carrots, the leek and the bouquet garni.
Strain and transfer the veal, mushrooms and white onions to a heated platter.
Reserve the cooking liquor.

In a heavy, medium size saucepan, melt the remaining 4 tablespoons butter over medium heat.
As soon as the butter begins to foam, add the flour and cook the "roux", uncovered, for 3 minutes, while stirring constantly.

Remove the saucepan from the heat.
Add one cup of the reserved cooking liquor to the "roux" and blend in well with a wooden spoon.
Return the saucepan to the top of the stove over low heat.
Add the remaining cooking liquor, one cup at a time, while stirring constantly.
Season with salt and pepper.

In a small bowl, mix the egg yolk and heavy cream together and whisk this mixture into the sauce.

Add the veal and vegetables to the sauce and rewarm for a few minutes.

Garnish with the chopped parsley.

145
Stuffed Paupiettes of Veal

For 4 people

---

4 6-OUNCE VEAL CUTLETS
SALT
FRESHLY GROUND PEPPER
½ CUP STUFFING [*Recipe 6*]
1 CUP FLOUR
3 TABLESPOONS BUTTER
1 TABLESPOON CHOPPED CARROTS
1 TABLESPOON CHOPPED ONIONS
1 TABLESPOON CHOPPED CELERY
¼ TEASPOON OREGANO
1½ CUPS HOT TOMATO SAUCE [*Recipe 33*]

Preheat the oven to 300°.

One by one, place each veal cutlet between 2 sheets of aluminium foil.
Pound each cutlet with a meat cleaver, until thin.

Season each cutlet with salt and pepper, and place 2 tablespoons of stuffing on each cutlet.

Roll the veal over the stuffing. As you roll the veal, tuck in the edges towards the middle.

Secure the rolls with white kitchen string.

Season the rolls with salt and pepper, dip the rolls in flour, and shake off the excess flour.

In a sauté pan with an ovenproof or metal handle, melt the butter over high heat until it begins to foam.

Add the veal rolls, reduce the heat to medium and brown the veal rolls.

Season the veal with salt and pepper.

Add the chopped carrots, onions and celery, and the oregano and cook, uncovered, for 3 minutes.

Pour in the tomato sauce.

Bring the sauce to a boil, cover, and place in the oven for 15 minutes.

Serve the paupiettes with rice.

146
Croquettes of Veal

For 4 people

  I POUND LEFTOVER COOKED VEAL, MINCED*
  I TABLESPOON BUTTER
  2 DRIED SHALLOTS, FINELY CHOPPED
½ CUP MUSHROOMS, FINELY CHOPPED
     SALT
     FRESHLY GROUND PEPPER
     PINCH OF NUTMEG
  I CUP HOT WHITE SAUCE, THICK [*Recipe 25*]
  I CUP FLOUR
  3 BEATEN EGGS
  I CUP BREADCRUMBS
     PEANUT OIL IN A DEEP FRYER HEATED TO 325°

AHEAD OF TIME: In a sauté pan, melt the butter over high heat until it begins to foam.

Add the shallots, reduce the heat to medium and cook, uncovered, for one minute.

Add the mushrooms and cook, uncovered, for 3 to 4 minutes, stirring occasionally.

Add the veal to the mushrooms, cook for 2 minutes and season with salt, pepper and nutmeg.

Mix in the white sauce and the correct seasonings.

Spread the mixture in a buttered baking dish and cover with buttered wax paper.

Refrigerate the mixture overnight.

Roll 3 tablespoons of the mixture at a time into the shape of a cylinder.

Dip each croquette into the flour, then into the beaten eggs and finally into the breadcrumbs.

Deepfry the croquettes, a few at a time, until golden brown.

Drain on paper towels.

Variety Meats

147
Technique: Preparation of Sweetbreads

Fresh sweetbreads should be washed in cold water until white.

Drop the sweetbreads into a stockpot filled with cold water, to which 2 tablespoons of white vinegar have been added.

Bring the liquid to a simmer over medium heat.
Continue to simmer, uncovered, for 8 minutes.

Cool the sweetbreads under running water for at least 5 to 6 minutes.

Remove the sweetbreads from the water, drain and trim.
Press the sweetbreads between two weights, for 2 to 3 hours.

148
Braised Sweetbreads

For 4 people

1½ POUNDS CALF'S SWEETBREADS
SALT
FRESHLY GROUND PEPPER
1 CUP FLOUR
3 TABLESPOONS BUTTER
2 TABLESPOONS CHOPPED ONIONS
2 TABLESPOONS CHOPPED CARROTS
1 TABLESPOON CHOPPED CELERY
¼ TEASPOON CHERVIL
A PINCH OF THYME
½ CUP DRY WHITE WINE
1 CUP HOT BASIC CHICKEN STOCK [*Recipe 17 or 18*]

AHEAD OF TIME: Prepare the sweetbreads, according to recipe 147.

Preheat the oven to 350°.

Cut the sweetbreads, at an angle, into 2 to 3 inch slices, and season with salt and pepper.
Dip each sweetbread slice into flour. Gently shake off the excess flour.

In a sauté pan with an ovenproof or metal handle, melt the

butter over high heat until it begins to foam.
Add the sweetbreads, reduce the heat to medium and brown the sweetbreads, uncovered, for 2 to 3 minutes on each side.

Transfer the sweetbreads to a heated platter and season.

Add the carrots, onions, celery and herbs to the sauté pan.
Cook the vegetables, uncovered, over medium heat, for 3 minutes, stirring occasionally.
Season the vegetables with salt and pepper.
Pour the white wine over the vegetables, increase the heat to high and reduce the wine for 3 to 4 minutes.
Add the chicken stock and the sweetbreads. Bring the liquid to a boil.
Cover the sauté pan with aluminium foil and place it in the oven for 30 minutes.

Transfer the sweetbreads to a heated serving platter.
Return the sauté pan to the top of the stove and reduce the sauce over high heat for 3 to 4 minutes.
Correct the seasonings.

Pour the sauce over the sweetbreads.

149
Grilled Sweetbreads
with Béarnaise Sauce and Watercress

For 4 people

1½ POUNDS CALF'S SWEETBREADS
½ CUP MELTED CLARIFIED BUTTER [RECIPE 13]
SALT
FRESHLY GROUND PEPPER
FRESH WATERCRESS AS A GARNISH
1 CUP BÉARNAISE SAUCE [RECIPE 34]

AHEAD OF TIME: Prepare the sweetbreads according to Recipe 147.

Preheat the oven to 350°.

Dip the sweetbreads into the melted, clarified butter and place them in a baking dish.

Season the sweetbreads with salt and pepper and place in the oven for 35 minutes.
Baste frequently with clarified butter.

Arrange the sweetbreads on a heated serving platter.
Decorate with the fresh watercress.

Serve the sweetbreads with béarnaise sauce.

150
Veal Kidneys with Madeira Wine

For 2 people

- 3 VEAL KIDNEYS, PEELED AND TRIMMED OF FAT
- 2 TABLESPOONS CLARIFIED BUTTER
- SALT
- FRESHLY GROUND PEPPER
- 1/2 POUND MUSHROOMS, CUT INTO 4
- 1 DRIED SHALLOT, FINELY CHOPPED
- 1 CUP HOT BASIC BROWN SAUCE THIN [*Recipe 28*]
- 1/2 CUP MADEIRA WINE
- A DASH OF CAYENNE PEPPER
- 1 TABLESPOON HEAVY CREAM [OPTIONAL]
- 1 TABLESPOON FRESH PARSLEY, FINELY CHOPPED

Cut the kidneys into very thin slices.

In a sauté pan, melt the clarified butter over high heat.

When the butter is very hot, add the kidney slices and sauté them for 3 to 4 minutes on each side.
Season the kidney slices with salt and pepper and transfer them to a heated platter.

Add the mushrooms and the shallots to the sauté pan and cook over high heat, uncovered, for 4 minutes, stirring frequently.

Add the brown sauce and the madeira wine.
Bring the sauce to a boil, reduce the heat to medium and simmer for a few minutes.
Season the sauce with cayenne pepper, salt and freshly ground pepper.

Mix the kidney slices and the cream into the sauce.

Garnish with chopped parsley.

151
Technique: Preparation of Calf's Brains

In a large stockpot, prepare a court bouillon consisting of:

---

10 CUPS WATER
3 TABLESPOONS WHITE VINEGAR
1 TEASPOON SALT
20 WHOLE PEPPERCORNS
2 BAY LEAVES
½ TEASPOON THYME
½ CUP SLICED CARROTS
¼ CUP SLICED ONIONS
2 WHOLE CLOVES

Bring the court bouillon to a boil and simmer for 1½ hours.
Very gently remove the membrane covering the calf's brains.

Gently slide the calf's brains into the court bouillon and simmer over low heat for 10 minutes.

Cool the calf's brains under running water for at least 5 to 6 minutes.

Drain the calf's brains.

152
Calf's Brains with Capers

For 4 people

---

4 8-OUNCE CALF'S BRAINS, SLIT IN HALF
SALT
FRESHLY GROUND PEPPER
2½ TABLESPOONS CLARIFIED BUTTER
2 TABLESPOONS BUTTER
1 TABLESPOON CAPERS
1 TABLESPOON FRESH PARSLEY, FINELY CHOPPED
JUICE OF ½ LEMON

AHEAD OF TIME: Prepare the calf's brains according to Recipe 151.

Season the calf's brains with salt and pepper.

Melt the clarified butter in a sauté pan over high heat.
When the butter is hot, add the calf's brains, reduce the heat to medium and cook, uncovered, for 4 minutes on each side.

Transfer the calf's brains to a heated serving platter.

Discard the fat from the sauté pan.
Melt 2 tablespoons fresh butter in the sauté pan over medium heat.

As soon as the butter begins to foam, add the capers and the parsley and cook for one minute.

Squeeze the lemon juice into this sauce and season with salt and pepper.

Pour the sauce over the calf's brains.

153
Calf's Liver, English Style

For 4 people

1¾ POUNDS CALF'S LIVER
1 CUP FLOUR
SALT
FRESHLY GROUND PEPPER
2 TABLESPOONS BUTTER
1 TABLESPOON VEGETABLE OIL
JUICE OF ¼ LEMON
1 TABLESPOON FRESH PARSLEY, FINELY CHOPPED

Remove the outside membrane of the liver, and slice it thinly, at an angle.

Dip the liver into flour and shake off the excess flour.
Season the liver with salt and pepper.

Melt the butter and the oil in a sauté pan over medium-low heat. As soon as the butter has melted, add the liver and cook, uncovered, for:

3 minutes on each side: *medium*
5 minutes on each side: *well done*

Squeeze a few drops of lemon juice over the liver.

Garnish with chopped parsley and serve immediately.

154
Calf's Liver Bergerac

For 4 people

1¾ POUNDS CALF'S LIVER
1 CUP FLOUR
SALT
FRESHLY GROUND PEPPER
2 TABLESPOONS BUTTER
1 TABLESPOON VEGETABLE OIL
4 TEASPOONS SHALLOT BUTTER [*Recipe 9*]
JUICE OF ¼ LEMON
1 TABLESPOON FRESH PARSLEY, FINELY CHOPPED

Preheat the oven to Broil.

Remove the outside membrane of the liver and slice it thinly, at an angle.

Dip the liver in flour and shake off the excess flour.
Season the liver with salt and pepper.

Melt the butter and the oil in a sauté pan over medium-low heat.
As soon as the butter has melted, add the liver and cook, uncovered, for:

   3 minutes on each side: *medium*
   5 minutes on each side: *well done*

Arrange the liver in a baking dish.
Dot the liver with the shallot butter.

Broil the liver, 6" away from the broiling element, until the shallot butter has melted.

Squeeze a few drops of lemon juice over the liver.
Garnish with chopped parsley and serve immediately.

155
Calf's Liver on Skewers

For 4 people

1½ POUNDS CALF'S LIVER
1 TABLESPOON BUTTER
16 MUSHROOM CAPS
4 SLICES BACON, CUT INTO 4
¼ CUP CLARIFIED BUTTER [*Recipe 13*]
SALT
FRESHLY GROUND PEPPER
½ CUP BREADCRUMBS
PARSLEY SPRIGS OR
FRESH WATERCRESS AS A GARNISH

Preheat the oven to Broil.

Remove the outside membrane of the liver and cut the liver into 2" squares.

In a sauté pan, melt 1 tablespoon butter over high heat until it begins to foam.
Add the liver and the mushroom caps, reduce the heat to medium and cook, uncovered, for 2 to 3 minutes.
Drain the liver and mushroom caps on paper towels.

Alternate the liver, mushroom caps and bacon on 4 skewers.
Brush the brochettes with clarified butter. Season.
Roll the brochettes in breadcrumbs.

Broil the brochettes, 6" away from the broiling element, for 3 to 4 minutes on each side.

Decorate the brochettes with parsley sprigs or fresh watercress, and serve with rice.

Rice

156

Rice Pilaf

For 4 people

---

    1 CUP LONG GRAIN CONVERTED RICE
    1 TABLESPOON BUTTER
    1 TABLESPOON ONION, FINELY CHOPPED
 1½ CUPS HOT BASIC CHICKEN STOCK
      [*Recipe 17 or 18*]
   ½ TEASPOON CHERVIL
      A PINCH THYME
      A BAY LEAF
      SALT
      FRESHLY GROUND PEPPER

Preheat the oven to 350°.

Place the rice in a strainer and rinse it under cold running water for a few minutes.
Drain and set aside.

In a heavy, ovenproof casserole, melt the butter over medium heat until it begins to foam.
Add the chopped onion and cook, uncovered, for 2 to 3 minutes, stirring frequently.

Add the rice to the onions and cook, uncovered, for 2 to 3 minutes, stirring frequently. Do not brown.

Pour in the chicken stock, add the herbs and season with salt and pepper.

Bring the liquid to a boil over high heat.

Cover the casserole and place it in the oven for 18 to 20 minutes.

Stir the rice with a fork.

157
Rice à l'Egyptienne

For 6 people

  I CUP LONG GRAIN CONVERTED RICE
  I TABLESPOON BUTTER
  I TABLESPOON ONION, FINELY CHOPPED
1½ CUPS HOT BASIC CHICKEN STOCK
    [*Recipe 17 or 18*]
  ½ TEASPOON CHERVIL
    A PINCH THYME
    A BAY LEAF
    SALT
    FRESHLY GROUND PEPPER
  2 TABLESPOONS VEGETABLE OIL
  ⅓ CUP DICED CHICKEN LIVER
  ⅓ CUP DICED COOKED HAM
  ⅓ CUP SLICED MUSHROOMS

Preheat the oven to 350°.

Place the rice in a strainer and rinse it under cold running water for a few minutes.
Drain and set aside.

In a heavy, ovenproof casserole, melt the butter over medium heat until it begins to foam.
Add the chopped onion and cook, uncovered, for 2 to 3 minutes, stirring frequently.
Add the rice to the onions and cook, uncovered, for 2 to 3 minutes, stirring frequently.

Pour in the chicken stock, add the herbs and season with salt and pepper.
Bring the liquid to a boil over high heat.
Cover the casserole and place it in the oven for 10 minutes.

While the rice is in the oven, place the oil in a sauté pan, over high heat.
When the oil is hot, add the liver and the ham, reduce the heat to medium and cook, uncovered, for 2 to 3 minutes.
Add the mushrooms and cook, uncovered, for another 2 to 3 minutes.
Season to taste and remove the sauté pan from the heat.

After the rice has been in the oven for 10 minutes, mix in the contents of the sauté pan.
Cover and return the casserole to the oven for 8 to 10 minutes.

158
Rice à la Grecque

For 6 people

---

1 CUP LONG GRAIN CONVERTED RICE
1 TABLESPOON BUTTER
1 TABLESPOON ONION FINELY CHOPPED
1½ CUPS HOT BASIC CHICKEN STOCK
   [*Recipe 17 or 18*]
½ TEASPOON CHERVIL
A PINCH OF THYME
A BAY LEAF
SALT
FRESHLY GROUND PEPPER
2 PORK SAUSAGES
1 TABLESPOON VEGETABLE OIL

Preheat the oven to 350°.

Drop the pork sausages into a saucepan three-quarters filled with

boiling water and cook, uncovered, for 5 minutes, over very high heat.
Drain, and set aside.

Place the rice in a strainer and rinse it under cold running water for a few minutes.
Drain and set aside.

In a heavy, ovenproof casserole, melt the butter over medium heat until it begins to foam.
Add the chopped onion and cook, uncovered, for 2 to 3 minutes, stirring frequently.
Add the rice to the onions and cook, uncovered, for 2 to 2 minutes, stirring frequently.

Pour in the chicken stock, add the herbs and season with salt and pepper.
Bring the liquid to a boil over high heat.
Cover the casserole and place it in the oven for 10 minutes.

Cut the pork sausages into ½" pieces.
While the rice is in the oven, place the oil in a sauté pan over high heat.
When the oil is hot, add the sliced pork sausages.
Reduce the heat to medium and cook, uncovered, for 3 to 4 minutes.

After the rice has been in the oven for 10 minutes, mix in the pork sausages.
Cover and return the casserole to the oven for 8 to 10 minutes.

159
Rice, Chinese Style

For 6 people

1 CUP RICE
COLD WATER

Place the rice in a strainer and rinse it under cold running water for 5 minutes.

Place the rice in a medium size saucepan.

Add cold water to one inch above the level of rice.

Bring the water to a boil over high heat.

Cover, reduce the heat to low and cook for 25 minutes.

Remove the saucepan from the heat and let stand for 5 minutes.

Salads

160
Caesar Salad

For 4 people

---

2 HEADS OF ROMAINE LETTUCE, CLEANED
1 EGG
1 GARLIC CLOVE PEELED AND SPLIT IN TWO
  SALT
  FRESHLY GROUND PEPPER
15 ANCHOVY FILLETS DRAINED AND CHOPPED
6 TABLESPOONS GRATED PARMESAN CHEESE
2 CUPS ONION AND GARLIC CROUTONS
DRESSING:
  JUICE OF 2½ LEMONS
5 TO 6 TABLESPOONS OLIVE OIL
    A FEW DROPS WORCESTERSHIRE SAUCE OR
      ½ CUP FRENCH DRESSING [*Recipes 37 or 38*]

Discard the wilted outside leaves of the lettuce.
Dry the lettuce leaves in a lettuce spin-drier or with paper towels and set aside.

Gently lower the egg into a saucepan filled with boiling water and simmer for 30 seconds. This is called to "coddle an egg". Cool the egg under running water and set aside.

Rub the salad bowl with the two pieces of garlic. Discard the garlic after use.

Break the lettuce leaves into bite-size pieces in the salad bowl. Season with salt and pepper. Mix in the anchovies. Break the coddled egg into the salad and blend well. Mix in the croutons and the cheese.

Mix in the salad dressing and correct the seasonings.

161
The Everyday Salad
For 4 people

---

2 HEADS OF BOSTON LETTUCE, CLEANED
2 HARD BOILED EGGS, SHELLED AND CUT IN FOUR
6 ANCHOVY FILETS, DRAINED AND CHOPPED
1 TABLESPOON FRESH PARSLEY, FINELY CHOPPED
2 TOMATOES, CUT INTO WEDGES
2 COOKED CHICKEN BREASTS,
      SKINNED, DEBONED AND CUT INTO 2" PIECES
   SALT
   FRESHLY GROUND PEPPER
½ CUP VINAIGRETTE [*Recipe 37*]

Discard the wilted outside leaves of the lettuce.
Dry the lettuce leaves in a lettuce spin-drier or with paper towels.
Break the lettuce leaves into bite-size pieces.

Mix all the ingredients except the salt, pepper and vinaigrette together in a wooden salad bowl.

Season the salad to taste.

Add the vinaigrette.

162
Pol's Potato Salad

For 4 people

---

4 MEDIUM-SIZE POTATOES, SCRUBBED
1 TABLESPOON FRESH CHIVES, FINELY CHOPPED
2 TABLESPOONS WINE VINEGAR
4 TABLESPOONS OLIVE OIL
1 TABLESPOON ONIONS, FINELY CHOPPED
   SALT
   FRESHLY GROUND PEPPER

Drop the potatoes into a large saucepan three-quarters filled with boiling, salted water and cook over high heat.
When the potatoes are cooked, transfer them to a large, heavy saucepan and dry the outside of the potatoes over medium heat.

Remove the saucepan from the heat and set aside for 15 minutes.

Peel the potatoes (Careful! They are still hot)
Cut the potatoes into large cubes.

Place all the ingredients, including the potatoes, in a bowl; mix well.
Cover the potato salad with wax paper and refrigerate for at least 4 hours.

163
Tomato Salad

For 4 people

---

4 LARGE TOMATOES, THINLY SLICED
1 TABLESPOON FRESH PARSLEY, FINELY CHOPPED
1 DRIED SHALLOT, FINELY CHOPPED
  SALT
  FRESHLY GROUND PEPPER
2 TABLESPOONS WINE VINEGAR
5 TABLESPOONS OLIVE OIL

Arrange the tomatoes on a serving platter.

Mix the remaining ingredients together and pour them over the tomatoes.

Let stand for one hour.

Hot Vegetables

164
Fresh Beans

For 4 people

1¼ POUNDS STRING BEANS, WASHED AND TRIMMED
 2 TABLESPOONS BUTTER
  SALT
  FRESHLY GROUND PEPPER

Drop the string beans into a large saucepan three-quarters filled with boiling, salted water.

Cover and blanch the string beans for 12 minutes.
Cool the beans under running water for at least 4 minutes.
Drain.

In a heavy, medium size saucepan, melt the butter over medium heat until it begins to foam.
Add the string beans, reduce the heat to low and cook the beans, uncovered, for 5 to 6 minutes.
Season to taste with salt and pepper.

165
Braised Endives

For 4 people

---

12 ENDIVES, CAREFULLY WASHED
4 TABLESPOONS BUTTER
JUICE OF ONE LEMON
1 CUP HOT BASIC CHICKEN STOCK [*Recipe 17 or 18*]
SALT
FRESHLY GROUND PEPPER
2 TABLESPOONS FLAKED ALMONDS

Preheat the oven to 350°.

Drop the endives into a large saucepan three-quarters filled with boiling, salted water. Cover.
Blanch the endives for 8 minutes, over very high heat.
Cool the endives under running water for at least 4 minutes.
Drain and place the endives in a buttered baking dish.

Dot the endives with 3 tablespoons butter.
Pour the lemon juice and the chicken stock over the endives.
Season with salt and pepper.
Cover the baking dish with aluminium foil.
Place the baking dish in the oven for 30 minutes.

Transfer the endives to a heated serving platter.

Place the baking dish on top of the stove over high heat and reduce the liquid by two thirds.
Pour the reduced liquid over the endives.

In a sauté pan, melt the remaining tablespoon of butter over medium heat until it begins to foam.
Add the flaked almonds and cook them until they become golden, while stirring frequently.

Spoon the almonds over the endives.

166
Mushrooms Provençale

For 4 people

½ POUND SLICED MUSHROOMS
3 TABLESPOONS BUTTER
1 DRIED SHALLOT, FINELY CHOPPED
1 GARLIC CLOVE, FINELY CHOPPED
1 TABLESPOON FRESH PARSLEY, FINELY CHOPPED
SALT
FRESHLY GROUND PEPPER

In a sauté pan, melt the butter over high heat, until it begins to foam.

Add the mushrooms, reduce the heat to medium and cook, uncovered, for 5 minutes, stirring occasionally.

Add the shallots, garlic and parsley and season with salt and pepper.
Cook for 3 minutes, uncovered, stirring occasionally.

167
Dutchess Potatoes

For 4·people

---

4 LARGE POTATOES, SCRUBBED
2 EGG YOLKS
3 TABLESPOONS MILK
   SALT
   FRESHLY GROUND WHITE PEPPER
   NUTMEG TO TASTE

Preheat the oven to Broil.

Drop the potatoes into a large saucepan three-quarters filled with boiling, salted water and cook over high heat.
When the potatoes are cooked, transfer them to a large, heavy saucepan and dry the outside of the potatoes over medium heat.

Remove the saucepan from the heat and set aside for 15 minutes. Peel the potatoes and rub them through a sieve into a bowl.

Beat the egg yolks and milk into the potatoes and season with salt, pepper and nutmeg.

Spoon the potato mixture into a pastry bag and form into the desired shape on a buttered baking dish.

Broil, 6" away from the broiling element, until brown.

168
Lyonnaise Potatoes

For 4 people

---

4 POTATOES BOILED, COOLED AND CUT INTO
   ½" SLICES
1 TABLESPOON BUTTER
2 TABLESPOONS VEGETABLE OIL
1 LARGE ONION, THINLY SLICED
  SALT
  FRESHLY GROUND PEPPER
1 TABLESPOON PARSLEY, FINELY CHOPPED

Place the butter and the vegetable oil in a sauté pan, over high heat.

As soon as the foam subsides, add the potatoes, reduce the heat to medium and brown on one side.

Turn the potatoes over, add the sliced onions, and continue to cook for 5 to 6 minutes.

Season to taste with salt and pepper.
Garnish with chopped parsley.

169
Parisienne Potatoes

For 4 people

---

6 LARGE POTATOES, PEELED AND SCRUBBED
4 TABLESPOONS BUTTER
  SALT
  FRESHLY GROUND PEPPER
1 TABLESPOON FRESH PARSLEY, FINELY CHOPPED

Scoop out pieces of potato with a round vegetable scooping spoon, making them as round as possible.

Place the pieces of potato in cold water and let stand for 10 minutes.

Dry on paper towels.

In a sauté pan, melt the butter over medium heat until it begins to foam.

Add the pieces of potato and cook, uncovered, over low heat. Stir frequently.

When the potatoes are golden brown, season with salt and pepper and garnish with chopped parsley.

170
Zucchini, Italian Style

For 4 people

---

2 MEDIUM SIZE ZUCCHINI, WASHED
SALT
FRESHLY GROUND PEPPER
PEANUT OIL IN A DEEP-FRYER, HEATED TO 325°

Slice the zucchini in half, lengthwise.

Cut the zucchini into ½" slices.

Deepfry the zucchini slices until golden brown.

Drain on paper towels, and season with salt and pepper.

Basic Doughs

171
Basic Pie Dough

Yield: two 9" pie shells

This dough is used for apple pie, quiche lorraine, etc.

2¾ CUPS ALL PURPOSE FLOUR, SIFTED
½ TEASPOON SALT
1 CUP SHORTENING, AT ROOM TEMPERATURE
½ CUP ICE WATER

Place the flour in a mixing bowl and make a well in the middle of the flour.

Place the salt and the shortening in the well and cut the shortening with 2 knives, or with a pastry cutter, until all the flour has been absorbed.

Add the water.

Pinch the dough with your thumb and index finger and form the dough into a ball.

Lightly dust the dough with flour and wrap it in wax paper.

Refrigerate for 3 to 4 hours before using.

This dough will keep, wrapped and refrigerated, for 3 days. It will also keep, frozen, for 3 months.

Return the dough to room temperature before using.

The pie shells should be baked at 400°, for 10 minutes.

172
Basic Sweet Dough

Yield: two 9" pie shells

This dough can be used for open pies, fruit tartlets, St-Honoré and sweet cookies.

2¾ CUPS ALL PURPOSE FLOUR, SIFTED
1 CUP ICING SUGAR, SIFTED
½ CUP UNSALTED BUTTER, AT ROOM TEMPERATURE
½ CUP SHORTENING, AT ROOM TEMPERATURE
1 TEASPOON VANILLA
2 MEDIUM SIZE EGGS, AT ROOM TEMPERATURE

Mix the flour and icing sugar together in a mixing bowl. Make a well in the middle of the mixture.

Place the butter and the shortening in the well, add the vanilla and cut the butter and shortening with 2 knives, or with a pastry cutter, until all the flour has been absorbed.

Add the eggs.

Pinch the dough between your thumb and index finger and form it into a ball. If you find the dough too dry, add 1 to 2 tablespoons of ice water and pinch the dough until blended.

Lightly dust the dough with flour and wrap it in wax paper.

Refrigerate the dough for 3 to 4 hours before using.

This dough will keep, wrapped and refrigerated, for 3 days. It will also keep, frozen, for 3 months.

The pie shells should be baked at 400°, for 10 minutes.

173
Creampuff Dough

Yield: 12 to 15 large creampuffs

This dough is used in the preparation of St-Honoré, chocolate éclairs, creampuffs, hors d'oeuvre.

1¼ CUPS WATER
½ CUP UNSALTED BUTTER
½ TEASPOON SALT
1 CUP ALL PURPOSE FLOUR
6 EGGS, AT ROOM TEMPERATURE
1 TEASPOON WATER

Preheat the oven to 425°.

Lightly butter a cookie sheet or stainless steel platter and sprinkle it with flour.
Set aside.

Place the water, salt and butter in a saucepan, over high heat.
Boil for 2 to 3 minutes and remove the saucepan from the heat.

Immediately add all the flour and stir vigorously with a wooden spoon.
Return the saucepan to high heat and continue to stir, until the mixture forms into a ball and no longer adheres to the spoon.

Remove the saucepan from the heat.
Add 5 eggs, one at a time, making sure that the dough takes on the shape of a ball and no longer adheres to the spoon before adding the next.

Spoon the dough into a pastry bag and form the dough into the desired shape, onto the prepared cookie sheet or platter. Leave at least 2 inches of space between the pastry puffs.

Beat the remaining egg with 1 teaspoon water.

With a pastry brush, lightly brush the top of each pastry puff with a beaten egg.

Place the cookie sheet or platter in the oven and bake for 20 minutes.
Turn the oven off.
With a fork, pierce the bottom of each pastry puff.
Return the puffs to the oven, close the oven door and let stand for 10 to 15 minutes.

Creams

174
Pastry Cream
Yield: 2½ cups

Used as a filling for pastry puffs, éclairs, etc.

I CUP MILK
I TABLESPOON WATER
I CUP GRANULATED SUGAR
3 EGG YOLKS
¼ CUP ALL PURPOSE FLOUR, SIFTED
I TEASPOON VANILLA

In a medium size saucepan, bring the milk and water to a boil over medium heat.

In a mixing bowl, beat the sugar and egg yolks together with a spatula for 3 to 4 minutes, until the eggs become foamy and almost white in color.

Mix the flour into the eggs with a spatula.

Add the vanilla to the boiling milk.
Gradually pour one half of the boiling milk into the eggs, while stirring constantly with a wooden spoon.

Return the remaining milk to the top of the stove, over medium-low heat.
Gradually pour the milk and egg mixture into the remaining boiling milk, while stirring constantly with a wooden spoon.

Continue to stir, over medium heat, until the mixture becomes very thick.

Transfer the pastry cream to a bowl.
Let cool and cover with buttered wax paper.

This pastry cream will keep, covered and refrigerated, for 48 hours.

175
Thick Custard Cream
Yield: 1¼ cups

This custard is served with cakes, ice cream, iced soufflé, fresh fruits and rice pudding.

---

1 CUP BOILED MILK, COOLED
4 EGG YOLKS
½ CUP GRANULATED SUGAR

In a medium size saucepan, beat the eggs and sugar together until foamy.

Mix in the boiled milk.

Place the saucepan on top of the stove, over medium heat, while stirring constantly with a wooden spoon.
Do not let the mixture boil.
Continue to stir until the mixture thickens and will coat a spoon.

Immediately transfer the custard cream to a stainless steel bowl.

Refrigerate the custard cream at least 24 hours before serving.

176
Chantilly Cream

Yield: 2 cups

---

    1 CUP HEAVY CREAM, COLD
    3 TABLESPOONS ICING SUGAR
    1 TEASPOON VANILLA

Beat the cream and vanilla until the mixture forms peaks.

Fold in the icing sugar.

177
Chocolate Sauce

Yield: 1 cup

---

    2 OUNCES UNSWEETENED CHOCOLATE
    2 TABLESPOONS BUTTER
    ¾ CUP ICING SUGAR
    4½ TABLESPOONS EVAPORATED MILK
    ¼ TEASPOON VANILLA

Place the chocolate in a stainless steel bowl.
Place the bowl on top of a saucepan three-quarters filled with boiling water.

Mix in the remaining ingredients.

Continue to cook the sauce, on top of the double boiler, for 20 minutes, while stirring occasionally.

Desserts

178
Iced Banana Soufflé

For 6 people

2 BANANAS

2 TABLESPOONS TIA MARIA

1 CUP MILK

1 TABLESPOON COLD WATER

5 EGG YOLKS

1 CUP GRANULATED SUGAR

2 TABLESPOONS UNFLAVORED GELATIN

½ CUP HOT WATER

2 EGG WHITES

2 CUPS HEAVY CREAM

A 6 CUP SOUFFLÉ DISH

Tightly secure a sheet of wax paper against the outside wall of the soufflé dish, with kitchen string, to 2 inches above the rim of the soufflé dish.
Set aside.

Peel the bananas and rub them through a sieve.
Mix in the Tia Maria.
Set aside

Bring the milk and one tablespoon of cold water to a boil, in a medium size heavy saucepan.

Set aside.

Beat the egg yolks and sugar together for 2 to 3 minutes, with a spatula.

Set aside.

Dissolve the gelatin in the hot water, in a small saucepan, and boil gently for 2 minutes.
Mix into the milk.
Gradually pour the eggs into the milk, while stirring constantly with a whisk or a wooden spoon.

Return the saucepan containing the milk and eggs to the stove and cook the mixture, over medium heat, while stirring constantly, until the mixture coats the spoon.
Do not let the mixture boil.

Add the puréed bananas and mix thoroughly.
Set aside until the mixture is almost cold, but has not set.

Beat the egg whites until they will hold peaks.
Beat the cream until it will hold peaks.
Gently fold the whipped cream into the beaten egg whites.
Gently fold the cream and egg whites into the cooled soufflé dish.

Carefully pour the banana soufflé into the prepared soufflé dish.

Place the soufflé dish in the freezer for at least 6 hours before serving.

179
Caramel Custard
4 to 6 servings

CARAMEL:
  ⅔ CUP GRANULATED SUGAR
  ½ CUP WATER
CUSTARD:
  2 CUPS MILK
  1 TEASPOON VANILLA
  1 TABLESPOON WATER

3 MEDIUM SIZE EGGS, AT ROOM TEMPERATURE
3 EGG YOLKS
½ CUP GRANULATED SUGAR

Preheat the oven to 350°.

CARAMEL: Place the sugar and the water in a small saucepan, over high heat.
When the mixture becomes light brown, pour it into the custard dishes.

CUSTARD: In a medium size saucepan, bring the milk, vanilla and water to a boil.

In a mixing bowl, beat the eggs and egg yolks lightly with a whisk.
Add the sugar and continue to beat, with a whisk, until well blended.

Gradually add the boiling milk to the eggs, while whisking constantly.

Strain the custard through a fine sieve and pour it into the custard dishes.

Place the custard dishes in a baking pan.
Make a "bain-marie" by pouring enough boiling water into the baking pan to reach halfway up the side of the custard dishes.
Carefully place the "bain-marie" in the oven.

Bake the custard for 40 to 45 minutes.

Remove the custards from the oven and chill before unmolding.

To unmold, lightly press the egde of the custard with your fingertips.
Place a plate upside-down over the custard dish, and turn the custard over onto the plate.

180
Cherries Jubilee
For 4 people

The Cherries Jubilee can be served over ice cream.

---

14 OUNCE CAN BING CHERRIES, DRAINED
¼ CUP GRANULATED SUGAR
½ CUP WATER
½ CUP KIRSCH
1 TEASPOON CORNSTARCH

Place the sugar and the water in a saucepan, over high heat.
Bring the liquid to a boil, reduce the heat to medium and simmer
for a few minutes.

Add the drained cherries and simmer for 2 to 3 minutes.

Pour the kirsch into a turkish coffee server or into a very small
saucepan. Mix in the cornstarch.

Warm the kirsch over medium heat.

When the kirsch has almost reached the boiling point, pour it
over the cherries and set alight with a match.

Serve immediately.

181
Chocolate Quatre Quart
For 6 to 8 people

---

8 OUNCES SEMI-SWEET CHOCOLATE
½ POUND UNSALTED BUTTER, AT ROOM
TEMPERATURE
4 MEDIUM SIZE EGGS, AT ROOM TEMPERATURE
1¼ CUPS GRANULATED SUGAR
1½ CUPS ALL PURPOSE FLOUR, SIFTED

Preheat the oven to 375°.

Butter a square 8" cake tin and sprinkle it with sugar.
Set aside.

Place the chocolate and the butter in a stainless steel bowl.
Place the bowl on top of a saucepan three-quarters filled with boiling water.
When the chocolate has melted, set the bowl aside and cool the chocolate for a few minutes.

During the time, break the eggs into a mixing bowl.
Add the sugar to the eggs and beat for approximately 4 minutes, until foamy.
Fold the chocolate and butter mixture into the eggs until well blended.
Fold the flour into the mixture until well blended.

Pour the mixture into the prepared cake tin.

Bake for 45 minutes, or until a knife inserted in the middle of the cake comes out clean.

When done, remove the cake from the oven and cool for 3 to 4 minutes.

Turn the cake over, onto a cake rack.

Let the cake cool for at least 2 hours before cutting.

182
Peach Melba

For 4 people

---

2 FRESH PEACHES, PEELED AND POACHED* OR
4 CANNED PEACH HALVES, DRAINED
½ PINT FRESH STRAWBERRIES, WASHED AND
STEMMED
4 SCOOPS VANILLA ICE CREAM
CHANTILLY CREAM, TO DECORATE *(Recipe 176)*

Reserve 4 strawberries,
Rub the remaining strawberries through a sieve.
Place a scoop of ice cream into each dessert dish.
Place one teaspoon of strawberry purée on each ice cream scoop.

Arrange a peach half on each scoop of ice cream.

Pour the remaining strawberry purée over the peaches.

Decorate with the chantilly cream.

Cut the reserved strawberries in two.
Garnish with the strawberry halves.

*In a saucepan, bring 2 cups of water and 1 cup of sugar to a boil.
 Carefully drop the peach halves into the boiling liquid and poach the peach halves
or 8 minutes.
 Remove the saucepan from the heat and cool the peach halves in the syrup.

183
Pears Hélène
For 4 people

---

2 FRESH PEARS, PEELED AND POACHED* OR
    4 CANNED PEAR HALVES
4 SCOOPS VANILLA ICE CREAM
    CHANTILLY CREAM TO DECORATE [*Recipe 176*]
¼ TO ½ CUP CHOCOLATE SAUCE [*Recipe 177*]

Place a scoop of ice cream into each dessert dish.

Arrange a pear half on each scoop of ice cream.

Pour the chocolate sauce over the pears.

Decorate with chantilly cream.

*See above footnote and follow same procedure.

184
Hot Sabayon

For 4 people

The sabayon can be served in small dessert dishes, or used to top fresh fruit such as strawberries.

¾ CUP GRANULATED SUGAR

4 EGG YOLKS

2 WHOLE EGGS

½ CUP DRY WHITE WINE

3 TABLESPOONS LIQUEUR, TO TASTE

In a stainless steel mixing bowl, combine the sugar, egg yolks and whole eggs.

Place the bowl on top of a saucepan three-quarters filled with barely boiling water.

Beat with a whisk for 3 to 4 minutes.

Add the white wine.

Continue to whisk vigorously until the mixture becomes very thick.

Gradually mix in the liqueur.

Serve immediately.

N.B. If the white wine is replaced by sweet marsala wine, the dessert becomes a "zabaglione."

185
Zambia Salad

For 2 people

---

 1 WHOLE PINEAPPLE
½ PINT STRAWBERRIES, WASHED AND STEMMED
    AND CUT IN TWO
20 FRESH SEEDLESS GRAPES, STEMMED
 1 ORANGE, PEELED, DIVIDED INTO SECTIONS, AND
    SEEDED
 3 TABLESPOONS GRANULATED SUGAR
 3 OUNCES KIRSCH
½ CUP HEAVY CREAM
 1 TABLESPOON ICING SUGAR

Slice the pineapple in two and remove the pulp.
Reserve the pineapple shells.
Cut the pulp into ½" cubes.

Mix the pineapple cubes, strawberries, grapes, orange, granulated
sugar and kirsch together in a mixing bowl.
Cover with wax paper.
Refrigerate and marinate the fruits for 1 to 2 hours.

Beat the cream until it will form peaks.

Fold in the icing sugar.

Spoon the marinated fruits into the pineapple shells.
Decorate with the whipped cream.

186
Zog's Baked Alaska

For 4 people

---

12 LADY FINGERS
½ PINT VANILLA ICE CREAM
5 EGG WHITES
½ CUP GRANULATED SUGAR
3 OUNCES COGNAC
2 OUNCES GRAND MARNIER

Preheat the oven to Broil.

Butter a stainless steel platter and sprinkle it with sugar.

Arrange 6 lady fingers, side by side, on the prepared platter, making sure that the edges of the lady fingers touch one another.

Carefully place the ice cream on top of the lady fingers.

Cover the ice cream with the remaining lady fingers.

Place the stainless steel platter in the freezer.

Beat the egg whites until very stiff.
Gradually add the granulated sugar, while beating.

Remove the stainless steel platter from the freezer.
With a spatula, spread one half of the beaten egg whites over the lady fingers and ice cream.
Make sure that all surfaces are sealed with the beaten egg whites.

Decorate the surface with the remaining beaten egg whites.

Place the stainless steel platter in the middle of the oven and bake for approximately 3 minutes, or until the meringue is light brown.

Remove the platter from the oven.

Place the cognac and the grand marnier in a turkish coffee server or a very small saucepan, over high heat.

When the liqueur is hot, set it aflame and pour it over the baked alaska.

Serve immediately.

Index

The number references in this index refer to the Recipe Number and not to the page number.

Ailloli sauce 39, 49
Alaska crab 116
Anchovy butter 11
Artichoke hearts 143
  (with veal)
Asparagus cream soup 67
Avocado 57

Bananas 178, 133
Basil - see introduction
Batters
  for deep frying 4
  basic crêpe 5
Bay leaf - see introduction
Béarnaise sauce 34
Beans (fresh) 164
Béchamel sauce
  thin 24
  thick 25
Beef
  bourguignon 125
  braised short ribs 124
  brochette 128
  club steak 119
  club steak au poivre 121
  club steak flambée 122
  flank (stuffed) 126
  fondue 98
  hamburger 93
  roast (how to) 118
  roast à l'Italienne 90
  sautéed with onions 87
  steak, Chinese style 120
  Strogonoff 123

stock (preparation of) 15, 16
  tenderloin 91
  top round 123
Blanquette of veal 144
Boeuf bourguignon 125
Bouquet garni - see introduction
  how to make (illustration) 16
Bourguignon sauce 30
Broccoli (as cold hors d'oeuvres) 46
Brochette (see Beef or Tenderloin)
Brown sauce
  thin 28
  thick 29
Butter
  anchovy 11
  clarified 13
  garlic 8
  kneaded or manié 12
  salmon 10
  shallot 9

Cabbage rolls 127
Caesar salad 160
Calf's brains
  technique 151
  with capers 152
Calf's liver
  Bergerac 154
  English style 153
  on skewers 155
Cantaloupe 58
Capers 152
Caramel custard 179
Carrot

chicken 130
cream soup 73
as cold hors d'oeuvres 46
Casserole
  halibut 92
Cauliflower (as cold ors d'oeuvres)
  46
Caesar salad 160
Cayenne pepper - see introduction
Chantilly cream 176
Cheese (see soufflés, fondues, ome-
  lettes)
Cherries Jubilee 180
Chicken
  à la Point 135
  Arlesienne 132
  casserole 130
  coq au vin 129
  everyday 134
  Kiev 131
  New Orleans 133
  roast 136
  stocks 17, 18
Chocolate
  sauce 177
  quatre quart 181
Chopping (illustration) - see intro-
  duction
Chopping block - see introduction
Clams (chowder) 76
Clarifying
  butter 13
  consommé 14
Club steak 119
  au poivre 121
  flambée 122
Cod
  au gratin 107
  à l'Espagnole 108
Coq au vin 129
Coquille St. Jacques 63
Court bouillon 19
Crab
  Alaska Crab legs 116

as hot hors d'oeuvres 53
Crêpes 5, 62
Croquettes 146
Croque Monsieur
  (see ham and cheese)
Cucumber
  cream soup 69
  in gazpacho 78
Custard
  cream 175
  caramel 179

Duchess potatoes 167
Duck
  à la Stanley Park (similar to
  Duck à l'Orange) 137
Dough
  basic pie 171
  basic sweet 172
  cream puff 173

Eggs
  français 79
  omelettes 84, 85, 86
  orientale 83
  scrambled 81
  with bacon and mushrooms 82
  with cream 80
Eggplant 132
Endive salad 165
Escargot - see Snails

Filet (in beef fondue) 98
Filet mignon 120
Fondue
  cheese 99
  beef 98
Food grinder - see introduction
Food mill - see introduction
French dressing vinaigrette 37

with garlic 38
with ailloli 39
Frogs' legs 117

Garlic butter 8
Gazpacho 78
Green beans 46
  (hors d'oeuvres)
Ground meat
  hamburger 93
  stuffed cabbage rolls 127

Halibut
  as cold entrée 54
  casserole 92
  poached with mushroom sauce
  106
Ham and cheese 50
  (hot hors d'oeuvres)
Hamburger 93
Hollandaise sauce 35

Kidneys (veal) 150
Kneaded butter 12
Knives - see introduction

Lamb
  shish kebabs 138
Leeks
cream soup 72, 71

Lettuce hearts 55, 90
Lobster
  broiled 113
  Newburg 112
Lyonnaise potatoes 168

Macaroni 89
Madeira wine 150
Manié butter 12

Marinades
  for beef, veal or chicken 1
  for lamb shish kebabs 2
  for barbecue chicken 3
Mayonnaise
  green 42
  plain 41
Mousseline sauce 36
  with poached salmon 105
Mozzarella cheese 50
Mushrooms
  à la crème on toast 88
  cream soup 68
  in an omelette 86
  with perch 102
  salad 166
  sauce 32
  with eggs 82
Mushroom caps
  cold hors d'oeuvres 45
  hot hors d'oeuvres 53
  stuffed with spinach and
  ham 54
  with crab meat 53
Mussels 66
Mustard - see introduction

Nutmeg - see introduction

Omelette
  art of 84
  cheese 85
  mushroom 86
  preparation (illustration) 84
Onion soup 75
Oyster (baked) 65

Paprika - see introduction
Pastry cream 174
Peach Melba 182
Pears Hélène 183

Pepper - see introduction
Perch 102
Pickerel 101
Plum sauce 43
Poaching
  halibut with mushroom
  sauce 106
  salmon in court bouillon 104
  salmon with mousseline
  sauce 105
Poissonière 104, 105, 106
Porgy broiled filet 109
Pork
  chops 141
  roast loin 139
  tenderloin (stuffed) 140
Potato
  cream soup 71
  Duchess 167
  Lyonnaise 168
  Parisienne 169
  salad 162
  soufflé 97
Pots and pans - see introduction

Quiche 94

Rice
  à l'Egyptienne 157
  à la Grecque 158
  Chinese style 159
  Pilaf 156
Roast beef 90
  how to 120
Roast chicken 136
Roast pork 139
Roquefort cheese (as canapés) 47
Roquefort dressing 40
Rosemary - see introduction
Roux
  technique 21
  brown 23
  white 22

Sabayon, hot 184
Sage - see introduction
Salads
  bean 164
  Caesar 160
  endive 165
  everyday 161
  mushroom 166
  potato 162
  tomato 163
Salmon
  butter 10
  poached 104
  poached with mousseline
  sauce 105
  smoked (as canapés) 48
Salt (sea) - see introduction
Sauces
  basic brown (thin) 28
  basic brown (thick) 29
  basic fish 27
  basic white (thin) 24
  basic white (thick) 25
  basic white (medium) 26
  béarnaise 34
  bourguignonne 30
  brown mushroom 32
  chocolate 177
  devilled sauce
  french dressing 37, 38, 39
  hollandaise 35
  mayonnaise 41
  mayonnaise (green) 42
  mousseline 36
  plum (Chinese style) 43
  roquefort dressing 40
  tomato sauce 33
Sausages 95
Scallops 63
Scampi
  au gratin 115
  brochette 64
  cold entrée 56
Scrambled eggs 81

Shallot butter 9
Shrimp
  how to cook 111
  preparation (illustration) 43
  butterfly 52
  cold hors d'oeuvres 44
  provençale 114
Snails
  au gratin 60
  bourguignonne 61
  provençale 59
Sole 110
Soufflés
  banana 178
  cheese 96
  potato 97
Spaghetti 95
Spinach (as hot hors d'oeuvres) 54
Steak
  Boston (Chinese style) 120
  Club (au poivre) 121
  Club (flambé) 122
Stocks
  basic brown beef, 15, 16
  basic chicken 17, 18
  basic fish (court bouillon) 19
  basic vegetable 20
Stuffings
  for poultry, beef or veal 6
  for sole, trout, doré, etc. 7
Sweetbreads
  technique 147
  braised 148
  grilled 149

Tarragon - see introduction
Tenderloin
  beef 91, 128
  pork 140
Thyme - see introduction

Tomatoes
  cream soup 70
  in gazpacho 78
  salad 163
  sauce 33

Trout
  amandine 103
  baked 100

Veal
  blanquette 144
  chops 143
  croquettes 146
  scaloppine 142
  stuffed paupiettes 145
Veal kidneys 150
Vegetables
  clear soup 74
  cold hors d'oeuvres 46
Vegetable stock 20
Vermouth 88
Vinaigrette 37

Water chestnuts 51, 55
Whisk - see introduction
White sauce
  basic from chicken stock 26
  béchamel thick 25
  béchamel thin 24
Wines (cooking tips) - see
  introduction

Zucchini
  cold hors d'oeuvres 46
  Italian style 170
Zambia fruit salad 185
Zog's baked Alaska 186

Illustrations

The food was prepared and photographed at the Pol Martin Culinary School. The lobsters were supplied by Gidney Lobster, 1855 Bois Franc Road, St. Laurent, Quebec.

Inside front cover photographed in the meat locker of N.D.G. Meat Market Ltd., 5343 Sherbrooke Street West, Montreal.

Cooking utensils photographed at La Belle Cuisine Cooking Utensils -- Helen Gougeon, 1200 Bishop Street, Montreal.

Spices photographed in the spice shop of The Main Importing Grocery Inc., 1188 St. Lawrence Boulevard, Montreal.

Cheeses photographed at The Cheese Shoppe Montreal Ltd., 611 de Maisonneuve West, Montreal.

Fresh fish photographed at Waldman Fish Company Ltd., 74 Roy Street East, Montreal.

Vegetables on back cover photographed at Gordon & Son Inc., 1208 Green Avenue, Westmount.

*Photography by Serge Beauchemin
with coordination by Christine Downs.*

Drawings by Betty Guernsey

*Designed by Robert R. Reid
Typesetting by Action Typography Ltd.,
Printed by Gordon W. Ross Ltd.*

A fish market
full of fresh fish
straight from the sea
delights the soul of
any good chef.